The HR Practitioner's Guide to Mergers & Acquisitions Due Diligence

Understanding the People, Leadership, and Culture Risks in M&A

The HR Practitioner's Guide to Mergers & Acquisitions Due Diligence

Understanding the People, Leadership, and Culture Risks in M&A

Klint C. Kendrick, Ph.D., SPHR

HR MERGERS &
ACQUISITIONS
ROUNDTABLE

The HR Practitioner's Guide to Mergers & Acquisitions Due Diligence
Understanding the People, Leadership, and Culture Risks in M&A

First paperback edition June 2020

Illustrations by Scott Allen
DealRoom screen capture used with permission

ISBN 978-1-7349583-0-0 (paperback)
ISBN 978-1-7349583-1-7 (ebook)

Published by Mergers & Acquisitions Roundtable, LLC
www.MandARoundtable.com

MERGERS & ACQUISITIONS ROUNDTABLE, LLC

Contents

Introduction

Working on mergers and acquisitions (M&A) can be both exhilarating and frightening. Even experienced practitioners with dozens of deals under their belt can be caught off guard and watch things go wrong, and people working on their first transaction can help ensure a successful outcome. The most significant difference between an experienced practitioner and a newcomer is the ability to tap into the lessons learned on prior deals and use them to direct their efforts toward a more favorable outcome earlier in the process. By reading this book, I hope that you'll be able to take some of the lessons I've learned and apply them to your own M&As.

I've been part of several poorly executed M&As in my life and have been acquired three times in my career. One of those times, I left the job—taking a significant book of business with me! I resigned because my compensation plan in the new company had changed so dramatically that I wouldn't have been able to pay my necessary monthly living expenses under the new quarterly bonus structure. Another time I discovered our company had made an acquisition when an acquired employee called me to ask if he still had a job! Since then, I've been responsible for helping repair several mergers that weren't well integrated, meaning those firms suffered lost productivity and profitability for years until the company finally paid somebody to clean up the mess.

I've also been part of many well-executed transactions and have learned from several phenomenal HR practitioners who cared deeply about their companies and the employees they served. This experience gave me a foundation for successfully leading dozens of M&A transactions that affected employees in over sixty countries. I've learned many lessons through hard work and have honed my skills through

1

ample practice. While I still make mistakes from time to time, they're usually far from cataclysmic.

One of the mistakes I learned from came when I was the HR lead for my very first deal after the training wheels came off. On the day of the announcement, my team sat in a hotel conference room with all of the target company's employees. They knew something was going on, and the word had already leaked that a big company was acquiring them. I looked out at the employees, many of them wearing the target company's logo shirts, and welcomed them to their new team, just like every speaker before me.

I let them know my team would be helping take care of their questions. That despite their very reasonable concerns, the acquisition was good news because there would be no layoffs, our benefits were more robust than theirs, and we had a great bonus program. I answered a few questions and walked off the stage with a smile. "We did it!" I told the team over celebratory beers.

The next morning, we had a fire drill. The most critical technical person on the acquired team was angry. Not just mad. Enraged! He was infuriated! He threatened to quit right then and there.

What happened? It turns out we hadn't given him a retention offer, and he felt like he wasn't valued.

We had covered the founders, who were getting excellent job offers. We had also identified a few other directors who were getting generous stay bonuses. However, we had missed one of the most critical individual contributors. This agitated the employee. It turned out he was *the* most vital individual contributor. He was the guy who had written 90% of their source code. If we were going to make the product better within the 12-month timeframe, we needed him to stay, and we needed him happy! We had to react quickly and find a way to keep him on board. It took a few days, but we worked things out and he remained with the company.

Even though we held several talent meetings with the target company during formal due diligence, nobody ever mentioned this person. I suspect this is because he was socially awkward and tended to be a heads-down worker rather than a self-promoter, and his top leaders forgot him. I later learned that another team had identified him as critical but had never shared that information with HR amid the fast-paced deal.

After making this error, I added a new step to my due diligence process so I would never make that mistake again. Based on sound advice I got from a person in my network, I started to include a post-diligence talent huddle to my process. This step has made an enormous difference, making it easier to identify key employees earlier in the process. I've shared this tip with dozens of other practitioners who have also started holding post-diligence huddles.

I'm passionate about creating a community of first-rate HR M&A practitioners because mergers and acquisitions affect real people, their families, and communities. M&A upends people's lives, sometimes for the better and sometimes for the worse. As HR practitioners, we have a responsibility to understand how human factors affect company financial performance, which requires us to know and care about people. The better we are at managing our M&A processes, the better off our companies and employees will be.

John C. Maxwell, the noted leadership expert, said "a wise person learns from his mistakes. A wiser one learns from others' mistakes. But the wisest person of all learns from others' successes.[1]"

I try to be wise enough to learn from my own mistakes. This learning allows me to make new and more exciting mistakes in the future. This book will enable you to be a wiser person, too. I've done dozens of deals and have incorporated those hard-learned lessons into this guide. I hope that you'll be able to learn and benefit from my mistakes and successes as you read this book.

I also try to take Maxwell's advice and learn from others. Having a network of practitioners to learn from and can call on for help is incredibly powerful. I carefully listen when they share what works and what doesn't. I try to apply their great ideas to my deals and avoid the mistakes they are generous enough to share.

I'm such a firm believer in the idea of peer learning that I started several roundtables for HR M&A practitioners. As of this writing, I've instituted HR M&A Roundtables in Seattle and Chicago. The success of these roundtables encouraged other practitioners to create HR M&A Roundtables in New York, Dallas, and London. Because not everybody lives within a reasonable commute of these areas, I also started a virtual HR M&A Roundtable that helps practitioners around the world get better at managing the people, leadership, and culture issues that arise during mergers and acquisitions.

The HR M&A Roundtable's peer-learning model has been so successful that we created an annual conference where HR and corporate development practitioners can come together to share their successes and failures in a safe and confidential environment. The roundtables and conference allow us all to get better at managing the people, culture, and leadership issues that arise in M&A. To learn more about the roundtable, visit www.MandARoundtable.com.

Because of the extensive peer-learning network I've helped nurture, this book contains not only the fundamental lessons I've learned in my dozens of deals but also the most vital lessons others have learned in their transactions. It represents billions of dollars in M&A and hundreds of thousands of lives touched by M&A activity.

As I've worked to become the best HR practitioner I can be, I've listened to hundreds of stories of failure and success. The nature of M&A work means only some details of a particular situation can be shared. To preserve confidentiality and ensure my examples are useful to the reader, the stories in this book are based on actual events but may have been modified or combined.

While the knowledge in this book represents the lessons learned and best practices from a mountain of deals, it's not designed to be comprehensive or exhaustive. I created it as a guide for HR practitioners who don't do M&A all the time.

Because I've worked primarily for US-based companies, my perspective will be US-centric. That said, I've worked only one deal where every employee was in the US. The vast majority of the transactions I've been part of spanned multiple regions and countries. Where appropriate, I've made a note of the global considerations that must be taken into account for successful HR M&A due diligence to occur. However, I'm not an expert in HR or M&A in every country, and I'm not an employment attorney. You'll want to consult with an expert or local counsel before finalizing any reports or plans for your transactions.

This book takes a broad view of M&A due diligence, which has several advantages for practitioners who want to excel in their M&A work. People, culture, and leadership risks don't arise only during the formal due diligence period but emerge throughout the entire M&A lifecycle. Being attuned to these risks throughout the deal—and being aware of them even after the business has achieved its final integration state—

will minimize errors and maximize the success of the M&A in meeting its business and financial objectives.

In addition to looking beyond the brief period of formal due diligence, this broad view encompasses more than mere identification and assessment of risks. No due diligence process is complete without evaluating risk mitigation options.

This expansive view allows for a broad working definition of due diligence. For our purposes:

Due diligence is the art and science of identifying, assessing, and mitigating risks associated with an M&A transaction.

While reading this book will give you a better understanding of the overall M&A deal lifecycle, I spend most of the pages discussing the formal due diligence stage. I made this choice because firms have the most robust risk mitigation options in that deal phase. I discuss the six major areas you must include in your due diligence to maximize your chances of deal success and provide some tools and techniques you can use to make your due diligence process more effective.

The M&A process is complicated and it's unlikely that the average HR practitioner will have the time or capacity to do every step suggested in this guide. It's an overwhelming amount of work, and very few people who do HR M&A full time do all of these steps on every deal. We need to carefully choose and prioritize the areas we explore and the questions we ask, trusting our instincts about the environments we work in.

My goal is for you to be able to read the entire book in a short period and still feel like you've learned something. If you're new to HR M&A, I hope you cover the margins of this book with your notes and underline the paragraphs you'll want to revisit when you're working a deal. If you're an experienced HR M&A practitioner and have just one or two highlights in each section, I'll consider that a win as well.

Klint C. Kendrick, Ph.D., SPHR
Chair, HR Mergers & Acquisitions Roundtable
June 2020

Part 1: M&A Basics

Mergers and acquisitions (M&A) are an essential part of today's business landscape. Even in the face of economic uncertainty, many leaders see M&A activity as critical to their business strategies[1]. As companies mature their M&A capability, people, leadership, and culture are becoming essential to extracting value from their investments[2]. As the focus expands from purely financial indicators to the talent agenda, companies will need to engage people experts for their M&As to be successful.

The first section of this book will provide context for the M&A people agenda, explaining the deal lifecycle, the strategic basis for M&A, and other basic M&A concepts. Once we have established a baseline understanding of M&A, we'll talk about some M&A successes and failures, and how the people agenda contributed to these deal outcomes.

Chapter 1: The Deal Lifecycle

Before we can delve into the specifics of M&A, it's helpful to have a general sense of the big picture. M&A can be intimidating for people who don't understand how it works. It can seem like an arcane process that requires an MBA in international finance to grasp fully. In reality, it's much simpler than that. Buying a company is much like buying a house.

Buying A House

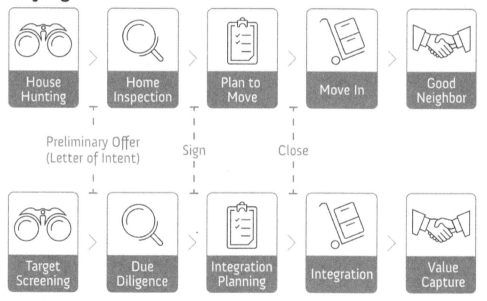

Buying A Company

Buying a house is a multi-step process that begins when the homebuyer decides they want a new house. They may choose to start the process by looking online, or they can secure the services of a real estate agent. They'll probably look at several houses, and when they find one they're ready to purchase, they'll make an initial offer.

In the world of M&A, companies frequently employ bankers and advisers to help find a suitable acquisition target. Large serial acquirers, such as private equity firms or businesses that continually make acquisitions, bring that expertise in-house. Even frequent buyers must occasionally partner with outside firms because smaller sellers will find their version of a real estate agent to help generate interest and get the best possible sale price.

Just as different homebuyers have unique real estate needs, the acquiring company will be trying to support various strategies with their acquisition. A homebuyer may want a starter home for their small family, or they may be nearing retirement and want a more modest condominium. A buyer may wish to purchase a duplex so they can rent out half, or they may be looking for a beach house or hunting cabin so they can get away from the city.

Similarly, the acquiring company's preferred target will change depending on how they want the M&A transaction to help them make more money. The acquirer may want to purchase talent (leading to what some call an acqui-hire), or the acquirer may be after intellectual property, such as a brand, technology, or specific process, like when Microsoft bought Skype[1]. A company may want to strengthen their supply chain, such as when a vehicle manufacturer purchases the company that makes their brake systems. A firm may purchase another product line they can sell with their current offering, like when Starbucks acquired La Boulange bakeries with the goal of offering better food to go with their coffee[2].

The buyer may be seeking market access in the form of new customers, new geographies, or other opportunities to grow their revenues. In this case, the company might decide to purchase a smaller firm in Europe rather than open a brand-new office there. Buying an already existing firm will often provide a more stable foreign presence than opening an office up on their own. In some cases, the companies may be headquartered in the same country, but have different customer lists. For example, TruGreen and Scotts LawnService merged in 2016, growing from the third and fourth largest lawn care services in the United States to the single largest due to the infusion of new customers[3].

For both the homebuyer and the acquirer, finding the right property to purchase is key to moving forward. Once homebuyers discover a suitable home, their agent will help them generate an initial offer. In

M&A, the initial offer is made through a letter of intent, frequently called an LOI. The LOI is non-binding but summarizes the proposed terms of the transaction. Discussing the most material items upfront allows the parties to determine if crucial terms and conditions are sufficiently aligned to move the process forward.

The primary focus of the LOI is financial terms. The purchase price is critical, as is the structure of the transaction, which includes whether the buyer intends to purchase all of the seller's stock or just select assets. The LOI usually spells out the next steps for the acquisition, including confidentiality requirements, use of advisers, and the overall process and timing. In addition to the financial terms, the LOI often spells out conditions for closing the sale (such as settling pending litigation or ensuring all employees have intellectual property agreements in place), treatment of key management team members, and how the formal due diligence process will work.

M&A Terms – Stock and Asset Deals

- **A stock sale (also known as an equity or share sale) means the acquirer is purchasing the entire ownership stake of a whole company. In a stock sale, the new buyer assumes all of the assets and liabilities of the business.**

- **A buyer who only wants part of the company will use an asset sale. In an asset sale, assets and liabilities are more specifically delineated. They may choose this approach to avoid assuming certain liabilities, such as those related to lawsuits, severance, or product warranty claims.**

After a homebuyer and seller have agreed on a price, the buyer will usually hire a home inspector. At the same time, they are starting to make their move-in plans. In M&A, formal due diligence is the home inspection, and integration planning is like move-in planning. This book will focus primarily on target screening and formal due diligence, with ample attention paid to how they affect integration planning.

Most real estate contracts allow the homebuyer to change some of the terms and conditions of the home purchase, or even back out entirely, if the home inspection goes poorly. The same is true of M&A transactions. The buyer can use their due diligence findings to terminate the sale or change the way the business is purchased. We will discuss options for handling due diligence findings in Part 4: Mitigating HR Risks.

Assuming both parties agree to continue with the purchase, the parties will negotiate the final sale and purchase agreement. The final contract is often referred to as the definitive agreement and is usually a complicated set of documents that spell out nearly every portion of the transaction. These negotiations often require several rounds of back-and-forth between each company's attorneys before they're ready to be signed.

One of the most significant negotiated points of the definitive agreement is the purchase price. The parties come to a fair purchase price using a variety of factors, including the value of assets and liabilities, an analysis of cash flows, and synergy projections for the final operating business. Human capital assets and liabilities would include things like pension and medical liabilities, unpaid employee entitlements, and the financial value of the company's talent. Cash flow should consider payroll and operating costs for the HR function. Synergies might include the future headcount plan, severance or retention payments, harmonizing compensation and benefits, combining facilities, and the costs and benefits of cross-training the existing workforces.

M&A Terms – Synergies

In the M&A context, a synergy occurs when the financial performance of the combined companies is better than the financial performance of each company on its own.

- **Revenue synergies happen when the combined company sells more goods and services than each company did independently.**

- **Cost synergies occur when the company spends less money to run the combined business than each company did separately. Firms often realize cost synergies through the reduction or consolidation of employees, real estate, and other business infrastructure.**

The definitive agreement may include employee terms and conditions, talent retention plans, indemnifications for legal compliance, and the cost of transition services. Transition services usually involve keeping employees on the seller's payroll and benefits plans until the buyer can establish payroll and benefits for them. We'll talk more about the definitive agreement in Chapter 16.

Just like a homebuyer can't remodel the kitchen until the sale closes and they have the keys to the house, the acquiring company cannot make changes to the target company until the transaction closes and they have full ownership. We refer to the final sale of the company as change in control. While it can be tempting to rest after a fast and furious formal due diligence process, HR practitioners should spend the period between signing the definitive agreement and closing the sale on planning the integration; just like the homebuyer should be arranging movers, talking with utility companies, coordinating major remodels, and deciding what color to paint the walls.

The timeline between signing the definitive agreement and closing the sale can be affected by multiple closing conditions, which are steps the seller must take before the buyer is willing to assume control. This process may include regulatory approvals or other compliance steps. Local law or specific contracts may require the parties to inform large customers, vital suppliers, or employee representative bodies like works councils or unions about the sale, or even gain their consent, to close the transaction. We'll discuss closing conditions further in Chapter 16.

Once the transaction closes, the seller will begin executing the integration plan they started to create during target screening and formal due diligence. The integration plan will vary by company and deal strategy as there is seldom a one size fits all approach to post-merger integration (often called PMI). Because so much of the due diligence process is context dependent, HR practitioners must truly comprehend the final integration plan. It's not uncommon for the integration plan to change in the course of due diligence, so HR practitioners must remain flexible.

Integration is where the company starts to capture the value of their investment in the new company. During integration, the focus shifts from risks to opportunities. At this point, HR practitioners must consider how people, leadership, and culture factors will make it easier for the combined business to make money and meet its other strategic objectives. This means that in addition to ensuring payroll and benefits are delivered to employees, HR practitioners should also consider organization design, retention and succession planning, communications, change management, cultural integration, and delivery of HR services to the new employees. Information gathered during formal due diligence will directly affect the integration plan and the HR practitioner's ability to execute on it.

Just like remodeling an entire home takes longer than updating the kitchen, the integration timeline will vary based on deal size and complexity. HR practitioners may be able to handle simple integrations in a matter of weeks, while others may take years and require large teams to manage. It's not uncommon for some elements of the business combination to be completed before others, making active change management imperative for ensuring employees are engaged and productive during the integration period.

While the home buying analogy isn't perfect, it can be useful for conceptualizing the critical steps of the M&A process and it is used throughout the book.

Key Roles in the M&A Process

Buying a home or company usually requires a team of people, each of whom has expertise in a particular field. Each company may use different job titles for each of the key responsibilities in the M&A process, but chances are good somebody is doing each of the jobs outlined below.

The **Business Sponsor** is the buying company executive who wants to pursue the merger or acquisition. They are responsible for understanding the strategy of their business and how the M&A activity will help the business grow. In our example, the business sponsor is like the homebuyer.

The **Corporate Development Team** is like the buyer's real estate agent. They find and evaluate companies that will help the business sponsor fulfill their strategic goals. The corporate development team will usually evaluate the target for strategic fit, create the financial model, manage the due diligence process, work with attorneys to negotiate contract terms, and bring the deal to close.

Some transactions will include additional outside parties. **Business Brokers, M&A Advisors, and Investment Banks** are like the seller's real estate agent. Each of these parties will offer different services, depending on the deal's size and regulatory requirements. Companies without an internal corporate development team may choose to use brokers, advisors, and investment bankers as buy-side agents.

Just like some complicated real estate transactions will involve lawyers, each side of an M&A transaction will use **Deal Attorneys** who specialize in M&A. Deal attorneys may include a combination of inside and outside counsel. They may call on other attorneys, like employment or intellectual property attorneys, to review certain parts of the transaction and represent the best interest of their clients.

The **Integration Management Office**, or IMO, picks up where the corporate development team leaves off. In some companies, the corporate development team and IMO are the same group of people. Think of them as a renovation project manager, who will guide the electricians, plumbers, and interior designers (functional experts) through the process of making the new home match the buyer's vision. The IMO is typically responsible for the overall acquisition project plan, managing the functional experts who will carry out the integration. They manage overall project milestones and integration costs and may also be accountable for realizing cost and revenue synergies.

Many companies will use **Functional Experts** to manage specialized due diligence and integration responsibilities. Just like a buyer probably doesn't want a roofer to retile the bathroom, the business sponsor probably doesn't want an operations expert doing HR work. Some functional experts may be hired from the outside, like a CPA whose only job is to look at the deal financials. Others may work on both due diligence and integration, like a supplier management professional who looks at the target's vendor relationships and then helps bring the vendors into the buyer's procurement systems.

Some larger firms separate HR due diligence from HR integration. This model allows the company to develop deep expertise in due diligence and integration, but risks losing the connection between the due diligence findings and the steps taken to mitigate those findings and ultimately realize deal value.

Due Diligence Happens in Stages

Most organizations take a phased approach to due diligence to ensure the process is confidential and efficient. Before an agreement is announced to the public, a limited number of people know about the transaction (M&A professionals often refer to this as being "under the tent"). M&A transactions are subject to strict confidentiality requirements, as the target company is often sharing sensitive competitive data. It could damage the target's business if suppliers, customers, or competitors discovered the company might be sold. Furthermore, if either company is publicly traded, disclosing the sale could create legal issues. Companies protect themselves against these risks by ensuring that only people who have a legitimate need to know about the transaction are aware of it.

A phased due diligence approach also makes the process more efficient. When firms are first assessing a target company, business sponsors and the corporate development team primarily evaluate the strength of the leadership team, market position, and financial factors.

Buying A House

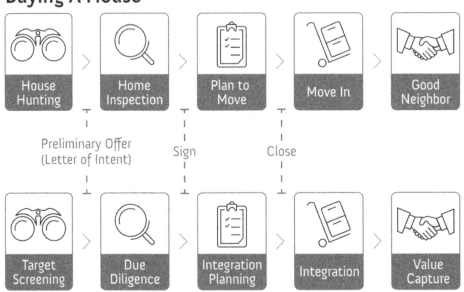

Decisions about the integration approach are not usually as relevant early on and expending limited company resources on a transaction that could fall through doesn't make much sense. Most of us aren't planning a wedding on the first date!

After the business sponsors and corporate development team make the yes or no decision, they will invite other people to participate in the formal due diligence process, and the range of concerns expands. The group of people who are interested in the M&A usually grows considerably as the deal moves from idea to reality. This book addresses a broad range of due diligence concerns, and each HR practitioner will need to determine which factors to investigate at what point in time based on their organization's norms and interests.

Each phase of the M&A process offers unique opportunities to gather information about a target company. Let's return to our house hunting analogy to discuss what information is likely to be available at what point in the process.

Target Screening

The first stage of the deal is frequently called target screening and occurs before the parties sign the letter of intent. This is the earliest part of the process and is similar to looking at homes and neighborhoods online, visiting open houses, and talking to the seller's agent. A potential buyer will only have access to a very limited amount of public information and a few seller-provided documents.

At this point in the process, the business sponsor and corporate development team are focused on a limited number of considerations that will help them decide whether or not to make a preliminary offer via the letter of intent. These considerations are usually limited to whether the acquisition is a good fit for the acquirer's strategy, the likely purchase price, and the target company's leadership capabilities.

The HR practitioner's primary job will be to use available information to find out if there are any deal killers, which are reasons the M&A should not go forward. This is when they should also start thinking about executive retention plans, which are covered in Chapter 18.

Many companies don't bring HR into the target screening phase, meaning the HR practitioner may have to play catch up during the formal diligence process. This practice is incredibly common, despite ample evidence that HR needs to be brought in at this point to assess people, leadership, and culture.

Formal Due Diligence

Once each side of the deal decides to proceed, more people and considerations are introduced into the process. The period between LOI and signing is sometimes referred to as formal due diligence. Think of this as a home inspection of the target company.

During formal due diligence, the target company will start to provide documents and make executives available for interviews. The acquiring company may also conduct site visits to see the target company in action. While the formal due diligence phase allows the opportunity to begin integration planning, most companies use this phase to validate the business, financial, and leadership assumptions made prior to signing the letter of intent.

At this point, the acquiring company will still be looking for deal killers and planning executive retention. The HR practitioner should also be ready to share any financial impacts they uncover along with any changes they think should be made to the final contract.

As we mentioned earlier, many companies do not invite HR to participate in the formal due diligence phase. If HR is shut out of formal due diligence, the firm will essentially be left to mitigate risks through the integration plan. Again, years of research and practice show that locking HR out of the formal due diligence phase is a terrible mistake, but some leaders need to make mistakes before they will change their processes.

Integration Planning

Just like most homebuyers are thinking about where to put their furniture before the home inspection is over, the HR practitioner should start thinking about integration during the formal due diligence phase. Remember, companies do M&As so they can execute their overall strategy. A strong integration plan that accounts for risks and opportunities will help the company make more money.

Once the contracts are signed, the deal is usually announced to the public and the need for secrecy is greatly reduced. HR will be able to ask more direct questions and start to coordinate more closely with the target company. There are laws about how much collaboration is permitted before the deal closes, so make sure the HR practitioner works with the deal attorney and corporate development team to avoid what the regulators call gun-jumping. HR will also continue to look at retention, but at this phase, retention will go beyond the executives and into lower levels of the organization.

Some firms choose to wait until the definitive agreement is signed before they bring the HR practitioner under the tent. If this unfortunate situation happens, HR will need to coordinate with the business sponsor, corporate development, and the IMO to prioritize areas for integration planning. HR should still spend time looking over important documents and learning about the target company, but the goal will be planning the organization's future state.

There is some natural overlap between due diligence and integration planning. In fact, some deals will have a simultaneous sign and close, which means integration planning must occur during the formal due diligence phase. This book will touch on some of the basics of integration planning and beyond, but they are not the primary focus.

Integration and Value Capture

Once the home sale closes, the seller hands the keys to the buyer. The buyer can then make whatever legal changes they desire. They may decide to move right in, or they could decide to knock down a wall and put a pool in the back yard. Similarly, the acquirer must wait until the deal closes before they can start changing things inside the target company. This process, and the final value capture strategy that drove the M&A to start with, will require a combination of common-sense HR, project management, and change management.

The integration and value capture stages are beyond the scope of this book, but HR practitioners are invited to learn more by joining the HR M&A Roundtable. You can learn more about the roundtable at www.MandARoundtable.com.

Chapter 2: Strategic Basis for M&A

Now that we have a mental model for M&A in general, it's time to get a better sense of why organizations choose to do a deal. Despite the oft-repeated mantra that "every deal is different," there are several fundamental ways organizations look at their M&A activity. For example, some firms look at M&A as part of an overall growth strategy, while others use it to strengthen their product and service portfolio in small but significant ways. Others use M&A as part of their alliance strategy, which is a way businesses cooperate for their mutual benefit.

This book provides some basic concepts, but to add the most value, each HR practitioner needs to discern how their organization views M&A and how inorganic growth is part of their firm's overall strategy. The most successful HR practitioners understand that an acquisition is one way of investing a company's limited financial resources. An organization will spend or sometimes even borrow money to make an acquisition. Cash paid for M&A means the company cannot allocate those same funds for research and development, the purchase of a new manufacturing plant, increasing total rewards, or creating a new marketing campaign. The choice to conduct an acquisition is an investment, and successful HR practitioners work hard to help the firm realize an appropriate return on that investment.

M&A Terms – Organic and Inorganic Growth

- **Organic growth refers to how a firm's internal operations expand revenue. Organic growth strategies include increasing sales with new and different products, improved customer experiences, or increased market penetration.**

- **Inorganic growth strategies include mergers, acquisitions, joint ventures, or other alliances.**

Earning a Seat at the M&A Table

Many organizations make a huge mistake and shut HR out of the target screening and formal due diligence phases, only letting HR know about the acquisition when the deal is announced. Most M&A research speaks only to the financial aspects of a transaction, despite decades of research showing that companies ignore the human side of M&A at their peril[1].

Even the most current M&A literature shows that HR practitioners have a long way to go before most of the M&A world will see us as adding value. In late 2018, one of the Big Four accounting firms compiled an M&A book that contains more than a dozen chapters and over 250 pages. Most of the book is about increasing deal value, but it only mentions acquired employees *three times*. Even then, the editors relegate employees to subpoints on deal valuation rather than recognize them as critical drivers of deal success. Warren Buffet and Jeff Bezos are each given more space than the thousands of people affected by M&As each year. It seems that no matter how much a company asserts that "people are our most valuable asset," the importance of people in successful M&A is underappreciated.

HR is often denied a seat at the M&A table because HR practitioners in the broader organization have not shown they understand how people matters holistically affect what business leaders care most about—the bottom line. To break through this, HR practitioners cannot afford to evaluate *only* basic HR processes, employee-facing policies and procedures, and legal risks. We need to understand how people will affect the financial success of the acquisition. We should show how our presence supports the deal thesis. The formal due diligence report and integration plans must reflect a sound understanding of how the firm's investment will pay off, alongside the role people play in the new venture.

M&A Terms – Deal Thesis

The deal thesis describes why the acquiring organization wants to buy the target company. A well-written deal thesis details the business case for spending money on the potential acquisition, expected financial outcomes, and how the company plans to integrate the new business so they can realize their objectives.

HR practitioners must have a clear picture of how the business works and how it makes money. We must be able to persuade business leaders that we grasp the way people, leadership, and culture affect the company's productivity and profitability. This collective HR challenge grows even more complicated in the M&A setting because the HR practitioner must not only comprehend how the acquiring business works and makes money, but we must also *quickly* learn how the target company works and makes money. Finally, we must have a vision of how the combined company will work and make money.

From there, adding value begins with understanding the strategy for the acquisition and is reinforced by demonstrating the ways people, leadership, and culture risks might keep the firm from successfully executing their strategic plans for the purchase. HR practitioners can take responsibility for in-depth knowledge of operational business elements, including workforce composition, total employment costs, organizational capabilities, and ensuring employees are motivated to fulfill the organization's objectives.

Successful HR practitioners help leaders systematically connect people and operational aspects of a transaction. We must equip business leaders with knowledge of the target company's performance before the acquisition and the steps they must take to ensure the workforce can deliver the same or better results after the businesses are combined. We must guide leaders through the complicated people, leadership, and cultural elements of the integration—on time and on budget.

Even when they know we can help, some business leaders need to stub their toes on problems we could have helped them solve before they invite us to bring our expertise. The chances of being invited to the due diligence process increase when leaders know we can help them improve business results. When we help the business be successful, we are credible partners who should be at the table.

Why Firms Buy

Firms choose to engage in inorganic growth for a variety of reasons. This section discusses many of the more common justifications for M&A. It's unusual for a company to undertake a transaction to meet just one goal. Sometimes deal objectives appear to conflict with one another, and other times it seems there's no strategy at all.

Furthermore, it's not uncommon for principal leaders of both the buying and selling organizations to have hidden agendas. Discerning the likely motives of both the buyer and seller can help HR practitioners more effectively shape the due diligence process from both risk management and integration planning perspectives.

Strategic and Financial Motives

Most people familiar with M&A think buyers fall into one of two camps, strategic and financial. While their specific objectives vary by deal, their overarching strategies for acquisition tend to remain the same. While we will talk about strategic and financial buyers' most typical motives for M&A, strategic buyers will sometimes do financial deals, and financial buyers will sometimes engage in strategic transactions.

Strategic buyers do deals to further their mission and vision. Strategic acquirers are usually companies that buy other companies to fold into their existing operations to some degree. Firms conduct strategic acquisitions to expand market share, gain customers, or obtain products, services, and expertise that are adjacent to their core business. Companies often cite growth as the primary reason for a strategic acquisition because inorganic growth tends to be faster than organic growth. The sudden introduction of new products and resources can make an enormous difference in the firm's top line and grow or die is a reality for most companies.

Financial buyers, on the other hand, do deals primarily to realize a financial return. Financial buyers are often private equity or venture capital firms. They usually buy intending to improve a business's financial metrics, like cash flow or operating margins. Once sufficient improvements have been made, they will exit that business through an initial public offering (IPO) or by divesting or selling it to yet another acquirer. Financial buyers tend to make up about 25% of the total US deal volume in a given year[2].

Both strategic and financial buyers have secondary objectives for their acquisitions. Most deals will have a number of these secondary objectives, and successful HR practitioners are aware of both the primary and secondary goals. Business sponsors and corporate development teams are typically more than happy to explain the secondary goals behind an acquisition. If you don't feel confident that you understand why your firm is doing a deal, go ahead and ask! Like we've all been told, the only stupid question is the one you don't ask. You have to understand what's going on with the acquisition to perform proper due diligence!

Cut costs. One of the biggest buzzwords in M&A is synergy. Recognizing a cost synergy often means the buyer is going to reduce spending through better management practices or economies of scale. In practice, this means the firm will consolidate locations, reduce headcount, offshore jobs or production, and take other measures to make the business run more efficiently.

The American Hospital Association reports a 2.3% reduction in operating costs when smaller hospitals merge with larger hospitals[3]. The hospital systems save money by purchasing equipment and supplies in larger quantities, getting the equivalent of a bulk discount. The combined hospitals also save money by having only one IT department which uses one data warehouse and one set of systems to conduct complicated patient analytics. They also benefit by having only one back office, which includes slimming down hospital administration, billing, HR, and other functional costs.

Increase market share. A company may choose to purchase a firm with a better distribution or marketing network. This strategy makes it possible for the firm to sell their current products and services to a new group of customers. Market share increases often result in a revenue synergy, which occurs when the acquiring company can increase their income by selling products and services from both companies to one another's existing or potential customers.

Charter Communications' merger with Time Warner Cable and related acquisition of Bright House Networks moved Charter from the number four cable provider to the number two cable provider. When sharing their investor presentation[4] with the market, Charter leadership touted 24 million customer relationships and a service network that would touch nearly every state in the union post-merger.

Expand geographically. Starting locations in a new geography can be a risky endeavor. Real estate, equipment, and labor costs begin to accrue in short order, but revenue takes time to materialize. There are cultural and regulatory challenges to address. It can be difficult to find leaders who can successfully work in a new location and are willing to move themselves and their families away from where they are comfortable and familiar. Purchasing a firm that is already successful in the new location can make it much faster to start offering products and services in a new location. Geographic expansion may also increase market share if the firm can introduce new customers to their products and services.

When international law firm K&L Gates wanted to expand into Italy, they decided to acquire a small firm based in Milan[5]. The acquisition was more efficient than applying for a business license, finding real estate, creating the infrastructure, recruiting attorneys, and finding new customers.

Reduce time to market or bet on innovation. Larger organizations occasionally struggle to beat smaller, more nimble competitors to market when consumers are ready for new products and services. These acquisition targets may be established companies with a new product the buyer wants, or they could be promising startups that have innovative ideas.

The 2017 acquisition of WePay by JPMorgan Chase bank is a perfect example of this strategy[6]. WePay was a leader in the growing area of online payment processing, with customers like GoFundMe using their services for online transactions. WePay had tapped a market the giant bank had not, and an acquisition made sense for a big company wanting to enter this segment.

Buy instead of build. Sometimes the costs of developing new technologies, products, services, areas of expertise, or resource pools are too much for a company to bear. Instead, the firm may buy a company that already has the desired capability at a price that is lower than the cost associated with building that competency in-house.

Walmart's acquisition of Jet.com gave them expanded e-commerce capabilities without needing to spend years trying to figure it out on their own[7].

Consolidate to remove excess capacity. Economics 101 tells us that too much supply means prices go down. A company may purchase an industry competitor so they can increase prices and margins, making it possible to generate additional revenues.

S&P Global Ratings believes two larger mergers in 2018 are the beginning of consolidation in the insurance industry. American

International Group (AIG) purchased Validus Holdings Ltd and Axa S.A. purchased XL Group Ltd. in deals worth nearly \$20 billion[8]. When large companies merge, they have less price competition, meaning insurance customers will probably pay more for their policies.

Annihilate the competition. The best way to drive a competitor out of business may be to buy them and stop offering their products and services. The results of an annihilation strategy are similar to the results of a consolidation strategy.

Apple paid \$3 billion to buy Beats in 2014, and less than a year later shut down Beats Music. That same year, they purchased music and podcast service Swell, which they also shuttered in 2015[9]. While Apple did keep some of the technology and personnel from these acquisitions, part of the strategy was likely closing down services that directly compete with Apple Music.

M&A Terms – Horizontal and Vertical Integration

- **A horizontal merger occurs when two firms in the same industry come together to meet several elements of a deal thesis. These include increasing market share, decreasing competition, diversifying product lines, realizing economies of scale, and augmenting talent availability.**

- **Vertical integration occurs when a company buys suppliers and distribution networks related to its current business.**

Real Talk: Political and Psychological Motives

As was just discussed, there are several logical financial reasons a firm might execute an inorganic growth strategy. These reasons are usually the topics of lengthy PowerPoints and complicated spreadsheets that demonstrate how the firm will benefit financially or strategically from the purchase of a company.

Unfortunately, firms often overstate the financial reasons to engage in M&A. Analysis of 60 years of M&A transactions shows that most deals have a negative economic impact on the acquirer[10]. Perhaps this is why Harvard Business School declares between 70 and 90% of M&As are not merely deficient but are "abysmal failures[11]." Within the first year of a merger, 90% of companies have lost market share[12] and revenue growth after significant deals decreases[13].

These financial realities mean we need to recognize the other political and psychological factors that are often at work in an acquisition. While this book will focus on the strategic and financial motives for M&As, HR practitioners will find it meaningful to recognize the multitude of other reasons a company may aggressively pursue a target.

One HR M&A Roundtable member who works in manufacturing shared an example of political motives for doing a deal. He was in a meeting with the corporate development team, helping them work through the labor cost model he had developed. After much analysis, the corporate development team conceded that labor costs were going to be significantly higher than projected due to automatic pay escalators in the target company's collective bargaining agreement. The roundtable member thought this realization would tank the deal, but instead, the corporate development person changed one of the revenue synergy numbers feeding the final ROI field. Playing with the spreadsheet, the corporate development team member continued tweaking the figures until the ROI calculation hit an acceptable level for the company's board to approve the acquisition. The roundtable member sat slack-jawed for a few moments until corporate development said, "one of our business leaders wants to do the deal, and he always gets what he wants."

I've heard variations of this story more than once—though we don't usually speak of such things. A 2016 Harvard Business Review article notes that "diligence work frequently results in an overly optimistic view of the revenue synergy opportunity.[14]" McKinsey research backs this up, with a survey showing that buyers only achieve 77% of projected revenue synergies. In addition to challenges measuring the actual impact, leaders struggle to shift the broader organization's focus and the sales team's behavior[15]. Competent people-leadership and updated financial incentives are often required to make these changes stick, making HR involvement early on even more critical to realizing the deal thesis.

Leaders may have mixed motives and reasons to engage in M&A transactions. Some studies reveal that management hubris can lead to poorly diligenced and executed deals. In these situations, the company may overpay and underperform in M&A transactions, presenting only flimsy financial justifications to the boards who approve the acquisitions[16]. Executives also find their personal fortunes increase when they manage larger organizations, which could incentivize them to do bad deals[17].

As far back as 1970, researchers saw how merely engaging in M&A was a good PR move for executive leaders. The choice to buy a company makes executives appear to be action-oriented leaders who take smart risks and push the organization into new frontiers[18]. The researchers noted that merely closing a transaction was often sufficient reason to attract attention from captains of industry, not only feeding the executive's ego but also lining their pockets.

These factors combine to show that engaging in M&A may have considerable upside for top managers. Unless the merger's results are catastrophic, a leader's reputation probably won't suffer. Research shows that well-connected CEOs who engage in bold M&As are more likely to receive CEO of the Year awards and substantial salary increases, despite destroying value[19].

Even Warren Buffet has his doubts that projected financial gains are genuine justifications for many M&As. In his 2014 letter to Berkshire Hathaway shareholders, he notes, "A lot of mouths with expensive tastes then clamor to be fed – among them investment bankers, accountants, consultants, lawyers and such capital-reallocators as leveraged buyout operators. Money-shufflers don't come cheap."[20] The Oracle of Omaha's annual letters to Berkshire Hathaway's shareholders contain a lot of wit and wisdom from one of the world's wealthiest men and most prolific acquirers and are recommended reading for any student of M&A.

This book focuses primarily on the stated financial and strategic reasons firms choose to engage in M&A. There's a lot to be gained by assuming the best in our colleagues who identify the target companies we'll be diligencing. That said, it's paramount to retain a high level of political awareness and more than a bit of healthy skepticism when working on transactions.

Why Firms Sell

Just as there are several reasons for an acquisition, there are multiple reasons why an owner will sell their business. The successful HR practitioner will be in tune with the motivations for the sale. If the seller's key executives are continuing with the company for the long-run or a shorter transitional period, understanding their motivations can be integral to retaining them and driving deal value. Additionally, the corporate development team will be working hard to convince these owners and executives that they should sell to the acquiring organization. These sellers may have multiple acquirers bidding for their business, and any contact members of the acquiring organization, including HR, have with the seller will help shape their opinion of the acquiring organization.

Smaller and Medium-Sized Businesses

The owners of small to medium businesses usually have different motives than the owners of larger institutions. In many cases, executives part with smaller organizations because the owner or board of directors wants an exit that delivers a return on their investment of time and money. Running a business is inherently risky, and when the company is mature enough to be sold, many owners choose to cash in on this opportunity before the market sees a downturn. They may consult with brokers and advisers to find the optimum time and ideal acquirer for their business to maximize the sale price.

Other owners find operating a business to be more demanding than is appropriate for their life circumstances. For example, they get sick or would like to retire. In cases like this, the seller often lacks a clear successor and believes selling the business is their best, or only, alternative. This approach frequently happens in family-owned businesses where the founder's children are either not ready or not willing to take over the company. In some cases, the owners would like to sell to their management team, but the management team is unable to raise or borrow funds to buy the firm.

Finally, selling to a larger organization may be an entrepreneur's goal. Many serial entrepreneurs thrive in smaller start-up environments and are excellent at growing businesses. These entrepreneurs have the skills to repeat their success over and over again. They sell one company and then use the funds from that sale to start another venture once the transition is complete. They may not, however, be a great fit for a large organization.

Larger Organizations

The authors of *The Granularity of Growth*[21] show how a combination of merger and divestment activity can help organizations create portfolios that contribute to market-leading growth. As part of an overall portfolio management strategy, strategic divestment can help a business focus on its core value drivers. By shedding companies or divisions that aren't part of an organization's grand design, the seller can stop funding activity that isn't getting them where they want to go and shift those resources to the parts of the business that are most critical to their long-term strategic plan.

Forest products company Weyerhaeuser used this strategy to move from a traditional pulp and paper company, exiting paper, containerboard packaging, hardwood, and home building businesses through strategic divestment. The company used funds raised from these divestments to pay off debt and purchase more timberlands and focused manufacturing facilities[22].

A divestment may also occur when a seller is choosing to remove their products and services from geographic or consumer markets where their products are underperforming or are at risk due to socioeconomic or geopolitical concerns. They may find they're overextended in specific regions or product lines and believe selling part of the business is preferable to abandoning it. Shuttering a business incurs hard costs like severances and can waste assets that might be more valuable as part of a different company. For example, an empty factory may have significantly less value when sold as mere real estate than that same land and building would be worth as part of a thriving business.

When InBev and Anheuser-Busch (AB) merged in 2008, AB brought a number of theme parks into the portfolio. Deciding that Busch Gardens and SeaWorld served a different customer market, InBev AB exited that market by selling the parks business to a private equity firm[23].

Companies may also choose to sell because they need to generate cash to pay off debt or because they want to engage in a new business strategy that requires more money than they have in reserve. In these cases, divestment may be a better alternative for fundraising than finding alliance partners, taking out loans, or courting investors. Campbell Soup sold several non-core businesses between 2017 and 2020, using the funds raised to pay down debt and realign the streamlined business for the future[24].

Finally, a company may be legally required to sell off part of a business that it acquired. When Albertson's supermarket chain bought several Safeway stores, the Federal Trade Commission dictated which stores they would need to sell off to ensure competition in certain areas[25].

Types of M&A Transactions

Regardless of the strategy for M&A activity, there are five basic types of transactions organizations use to meet their strategic goals. These are mergers, acquisitions, divestitures, equity investments, and joint ventures.

Mergers and Acquisitions

Legally speaking, mergers and acquisitions are different ways of bringing legal entities together. Mergers may have tax and legal consequences (including employment law consequences) that are different from the implications of an acquisition. The legal definitions, however, are not how most people look at mergers and acquisitions, and unless the deal structure affects the employees, we won't split hairs on the technical differences.

In everyday language, **mergers** are a coming together of two equals. While the marriage of two equals reminds us of the beautiful choice two compatible people make to spend the rest of their lives together, these are business transactions. The marriage of equals rarely happens in business, as there is almost always a more dominant company either financially or culturally. The dominant company's leadership usually remains in strategic positions, though the acquirer may place a few executives from the less dominant firm into token roles. Furthermore, the culturally dominant firm often continues its management practices in the combined company, despite promises to make it the best of both worlds. In short, the honeymoon is usually over quickly, and there is trouble in paradise if the merger isn't handled well from the start.

Acquisitions are similar to mergers in that two companies are coming together. The term, however, may be seen as more hostile. A common perception is that the larger company is taking over the smaller organization. With an acquisition, the dominant company's management structure and business practices usually remain intact. While a takeover is not always the case, as there are several different ways to integrate an acquisition, the perception is generally accurate. Sometimes acquisitions are referred to as mergers because it evokes the marriage of equals, but the result is the same—one company has taken over another.

Other Related Transactions

The next three transaction types are related to mergers and acquisitions but are outside the scope of this book. Knowing the basics of these transactions can be helpful for an HR practitioner who works for a company that is interested in growing inorganically.

A *divestiture* occurs when all or part of a business is sold to another firm. It is tempting to view a divestiture as the exact opposite of a merger or acquisition. However, nothing could be further from the truth. Divestitures are complicated transactions on their own and are frequently more challenging to execute than a purchase. When an HR practitioner helps with a business sale, they may be required to provide due diligence information to the buyer, so it will be helpful for them to understand the process.

An *equity investment* occurs when a firm chooses to allocate funds toward another business and its activities. A company may decide to do this if a critical supplier needs help, a startup shows promise, or they would like more control over how another business operates. Investors may choose to perform due diligence on an equity investment partner, but it looks somewhat different than the application we'll cover in this book.

The final transaction type is a *joint venture*, frequently called a JV. In a JV, one organization invests in a strategic partnership with one or more other organizations to pursue mutually beneficial opportunities. The investment can be cash, physical assets, intellectual property, people, or other assets. Companies can be majority owners, minority owners, or equal owners. With a JV, each company usually gets representation on the JV's board of directors and some direct or indirect control of the JV's business activities. Like equity investments, due diligence is often performed on the JV partner, though it looks quite a bit different than M&A due diligence.

Thinking About Integration

If the M&A transaction is like purchasing a house, integration is about what will be done with the house. Most people would naturally think about a home they plan to occupy differently than a home they are procuring to use as a rental property. An empty-nester getting a retirement home will look at their place differently than a couple expecting their third child. A property developer may not care about the house at all because they're buying a home to tear it down and subdivide the lot or build apartments on the land.

Making the most of a home purchase means knowing what's going to happen with the house. Similarly, making the most of the M&A process means knowing the final plan for the target company. While the exact integration model may not be fleshed out when the due diligence process starts, and will probably change as the acquirer learns more about the target company, HR should at least have a sense of the proposed end state to make the most of the due diligence process.

Despite this undeniable reality, one of the key challenges many firms face is the lack of a clear integration plan. While a clear end state is supposed to be part of the deal thesis, Harvard Business School research shows that nearly 40% of acquirers jump into a deal with no sound reason for buying a company. Another 30% find their justifications don't hold up for three years after closing the transaction. Fully 70% of M&A transactions lack an integration plan that will stand the test of time! [26]

In his book *Agile M&A*, Kison Patel cites several industry insiders who have seen deal teams make poor decisions about acquisition targets, leaving integration leaders to clean up the mess[27]. Throughout his book, Kison argues that seasoned acquirers see M&A as a complete project that goes from target screening to final integration. In this ideal model, each person on the team should help their firm achieve exceptional results through a collaborative effort. While leading-edge companies like Google and Atlassian can collaborate using the methods Kison recommends, that aspirational state is not attained by most acquiring organizations due to mismatched incentives between the dealmakers (who get paid to close deals) and integration leaders (who get paid to make the deals work out).

This lack of a clear plan makes it difficult for anybody, including the HR practitioner, to understand how the acquisition will provide a positive return on investment. The absence of a clear end state doesn't need to spell gloom for every HR practitioner working on M&A; in fact, it may provide an opportunity for the HR practitioner to shine. A keen understanding of the acquirer, the target, and the overall goals of the transaction can allow HR practitioners to help shape the final strategy.

One of our HR M&A Roundtable members was the HR leader at a high-growth startup in the entertainment space. Her organization had the opportunity to acquire a small online media division of a much larger organization, but the firm's leaders needed to make a decision very quickly as the seller was starting to market the firm outside of his small circle. The acquirer's entire leadership team came together to discuss the acquisition opportunity and whether or not it made sense to invest their limited capital on this purchase.

The HR leader asked several questions about the potential target's workforce and leadership. During that conversation, it became evident that one of the acquirer's senior leaders would need to be assigned to manage the new division full-time. Not only was the HR leader able to recommend an appropriate executive for the acquired company, but it also reinforced the value of the succession planning process she had recently put into place.

Common Integration Scenarios

In the absence of a clear and sustainable integration plan, the HR practitioner must make some logical guesses and be able to consider multiple scenarios. Many times, the risks will be similar enough between possible models to proceed with minimal disruption to due diligence.

A few of the more common integration strategies are detailed below. This list provides a starting point for considering the HR risks associated with a deal's post-integration model.

Remain standalone. Sometimes an acquirer will choose not to integrate a business at all. In this case, the acquired company will operate as an independent organization with its own goals, strategies, and business operations. Conglomerates, private equity firms, and other organizations that approach their holdings like a portfolio are most likely to choose this strategy,

An example of this is where an investor buys an apartment building but doesn't change anything about the way it operates. The property manager continues to provide support to the tenants and uses all of the existing vendors to keep the property in good repair. The only thing the property manager changes is where he sends the rents.

Partial integration occurs when the acquirer chooses to pull some functions into the parent organization while leaving other aspects to be managed by the legacy company. For example, back-office functions like HR, IT, and finance may be governed by the parent company while the leadership team that was in place before the acquisition maintains control of R&D, manufacturing, distribution, marketing, and sales.

In this case, an investor buys an apartment building and keeps the building manager in place to help tenants and collect rents but changes the maintenance and landscaping service.

Full integration occurs when the buyer absorbs the entire acquired organization into its policies, processes, infrastructure, and governance. This approach is sometimes called total assimilation because the target company's way of doing business is typically erased in full integration. Full integration is much easier to achieve when a more substantial organization absorbs a much smaller company into one of its already existing operating units (sometimes called a tuck-in). Full integration may also occur when the acquired company becomes a standalone operating unit that relies on the same governance models and infrastructure as the parent (sometimes called a bolt-on).

In this example, our investor buys an apartment building and makes it look like all of her other properties. The signage changes, the buildings are painted, the landscaper and other vendors are replaced, and a new team manages the property.

Business transformation occurs when top executives use a merger or acquisition to reinvent the combined business and make it more competitive. This strategy is more achievable when two organizations of roughly the same size come together through strategic merger or acquisition of a comparatively large organization. Business leaders can use the infusion of new people, products, and technology to help create the desired change.

In this scenario, the investor already owns an apartment building and decides to buy another one. The investor picks the best part of each location, choosing the best manager and vendors for all of her buildings.

These definitions are general guidelines that may not apply to every scenario. Different organizations have different ways of thinking about their integration models, and HR practitioners are encouraged to check in with the business sponsors and corporate development leaders who are making decisions about the future operating model so they can add maximum value during the due diligence process.

Chapter 3: What Makes Deals Work – Or Not

Global deal volume peaked in 2015, with nearly $2.1 trillion in aggregate deal value that year. In 2019, the most recent year for which we have data, total deal volume remained strong, with $1.8 trillion in aggregate deal value. Both mega deals (those over $10 billion in value) and large deals ($1 billion to $10 billion) neared records with 28 mega-deals and over 1,000 other transactions worth more than $100 million announced. Middle-market deals ($100 million to $1 billion), on the other hand, slowed to near-decade lows, but still totaled $258 billion in value[1]. Even with fears of a downturn looming, companies are sitting on more cash than they had in 2007, leading Big Four accounting firm PwC to believe that even turbulent economic waters won't suppress global M&A the way the Great Recession did[2]. At the time of this book's release, the full effect of the COVID-19 pandemic has yet to be felt and could greatly change the landscape.

Big transactions usually involve big names, making it easier to relate to some of the dynamics that happen in M&A. In this chapter, we'll take a brief look at some of the largest deals in history and how people, leadership, and culture factors uncovered during the diligence process led to their success or failure.

Deals that Worked

To start, here are a few classic examples of M&As that worked out well.

Disney and Pixar

The 2006 acquisition of Pixar by Disney for $7.4 billion is a lesson in how to manage culture in a deal. Three years before the agreement materialized, Disney and Pixar had talked about an alliance, but the clash between Disney CEO Michael Eisner and Pixar CEO Steve Jobs was too much to make the deal work. When Eisner left, and Bob Iger took the Disney helm, they discussed the merger again[3].

Bob Iger had already been through several M&A deals and understood some of the challenges that arise when cultures clash. So instead of completely assimilating Pixar, Disney treated their new acquisition as a mostly standalone operation. Decisive cultural identifiers, like email addresses, signage, and the casual dress code all stayed in place, keeping Pixar employees productive and engaged in their familiar work environment. After some time, Disney asked Pixar leaders to step in and turn around Disney's internal animation studio. Iger and Jobs had discussed this move during the early diligence phase, long before the final agreement was signed.

Since then, Disney has also acquired Marvel for $4 billion in 2009[4] and Lucasfilm for another $4 billion in 2012[5], using the same approach to managing people, leadership, and culture. While these moves have not gone without criticism, the box office power of Disney is undisputable, with seven of the ten highest-grossing movies worldwide in 2019 coming from the House of Mouse[6].

Google and Android

While Google has not officially confirmed the amount, most estimates place the 2005 acquisition of Android at $50 million. Over the next three years, Google invested in its new addition to create the most dominant mobile operating system in the world, with over 85% of smartphones released in 2018 using Android[7]. In the past decade, Android has unseated the Windows, Nokia, and Blackberry mobile operating systems leaving Apple's iPhone as its only competition.

The success of this acquisition wasn't an accident. Android's founders were a team of known technologists who had a track record with companies like Apple, WebTV, and Microsoft. The first meeting between Android and Google executives happened after the T-Mobile Sidekick, the first phone to use the Android OS, hit the market. While Google executives talked about the phone itself, the meeting was a disguised due diligence conversation focused on leadership and cultural compatibility, with Google executives probing collaboration and decision-making styles[8].

Google reports that two-thirds of their acquisitions are successful[9], a number that is staggering compared to the 70 to 90% failure rate reported in the business press. To make their deals work, Google focuses on ensuring they acquire companies with talented people who are versatile enough to work in many parts of the business, ensuring acquired leaders stay on board to see their projects to fruition, and support cultural realignment that makes the entire process smoother.

Exxon and Mobil

In 1998, Exxon and Mobil created the world's largest company in what was then the world's largest merger, worth a staggering $74 billion. Corporate consolidation was an ideal strategy for these two significant players who constructed the deal during a time of low oil prices due to oversupply in the market. The merger's financial plan, created during due diligence, called for the combined company to cut nearly 10,000 jobs and close several offices[10]. This task required involvement from a legion of HR practitioners to manage redeployment and office closures. Despite the controversial nature of this decision and the oil and gas industry's general practices, the merger was a financial success. ExxonMobil remains the world's largest non-government-owned energy provider, and analysts are bullish about its future.

Deals That Didn't Work

For every arrangement that works, there are three or four that do not. The examples below are textbook cases of failed M&As. These catastrophic failures occurred, at least in part, because leaders didn't have the information required to take decisive action. A due diligence process that appreciates the role of people, leadership, and culture would have better positioned executive leaders to create meaningful plans. Instead, executives ended up focused on people issues too late to keep the businesses from circling the drain.

Bank of America, Merrill Lynch and Countrywide Financial

During the Great Recession of 2007 to 2009, Bank of America (B of A) made two acquisitions that became epic failures. The first was Merrill Lynch, an investment that was encouraged by the US government, and Countrywide Mortgage, which was not.

The \$50 billion acquisition of Merrill Lynch was announced an hour before news of Lehman Brothers' spectacular collapse. Merrill had taken significant write-downs of subprime loans, just like Lehman, and the acquisition likely saved Merrill from a similar fate. On the day of the announcement, B of A's then-CEO, Ken Lewis, called Merrill's "thundering herd" of brokers the crown jewel of the acquisition, promising to use them to sell stocks to Main Street and not just Wall Street[11]. B of A's integration dragged on indefinitely[12], and B of A reneged on the "Wall Street to Main Street" promise they made to their brokers. B of A offered generous retention packages to top producers, but many of those just below the top tier left and took significant books of business with them[13]. By 2015, the brokers who remained were growing frustrated by the change from a customer-first culture at legacy Merrill Lynch to a bank-first culture that required them to send brokerage accounts under \$250,000 to a call center, along with measuring cross-selling referrals for mortgages and checking accounts[14]. B of A continues to downplay the Merrill brand, further frustrating some of their brokers and lowering morale[15]. These changes have left Merrill Lynch under industry benchmarks for customer satisfaction.

This deal is a classic example of psychological and political motives, rather than financial motives, driving a purchase. Lewis' mentor and predecessor had eyed Merrill Lynch for years but could never close the deal[16]. When Lewis saw the opportunity, he leaped without looking, uncovering significant problems only after B of A announced the agreement. Because they didn't perform proper due diligence, the warning signs came too late. In addition to valuation questions[17], Lewis learned about the new Merrill CEO's excesses, including expensive art for his office and astronomical pay packages for new executives[18], far too late to take action.

By the time Lewis decided to back out, the US government had pressured him to close the deal, concerned that Merrill's subprime investments would further damage the economy. The US taxpayer ultimately gave B of A a \$20 billion bailout package, which they eventually paid back.

Bank of America's failed \$2.5 billion acquisition of Countrywide Mortgage[19], a firm that wrote many of the subprime loans that brought Lehman and Merrill down, added to the company's problems. While official due diligence reports said it was a good investment, executives in B of A's mortgage unit believed Countrywide's questionable lending practices, driven by a problematic corporate culture, were ethically dubious and would ultimately cause problems because borrowers were encouraged to take loans they couldn't repay. These problems have amounted to over $50 billion in write-downs, fines, and settlements. The total loss was over 2,000% of the total investments, a combined 60% decrease in share price, and an indelibly tarnished reputation.

Daimler-Benz and Chrysler

The $36 billion merger of Daimler-Benz and Chrysler was seen as a triumphant comeback for America's third-largest automobile manufacturer, even though analysts thought it would be challenging from the start due to differences in culture and operating models. DaimlerChrysler would have two headquarters, one in Stuttgart, Germany and one in Detroit. German executive Juergen Schrempp would share power with Chrysler CEO Robert Eaton for some time. Executives selected London for the 1998 announcement because it was neutral ground, ensuring that neither executive upstaged the other on their home turf[20].

Unlike many mega mergers, which rely on cost-cutting to compete, Daimler wanted access to production capacity outside Germany. Slow-moving Daimler was also going to learn from Chrysler's ability to get products to market much more quickly than their plodding German parent. Daimler would give its Mercedes brand broader access to American consumers through the network of Chrysler and Jeep dealerships. Industry insiders thought a well-executed deal could help Daimler compete in a global market.

Like the B of A example above, both parties rushed through the due diligence process. The CEOs announced the merger only weeks after the they had met again at an auto show. Some speculate the rushed deal was a reaction to a prior takeover bid by billionaire Kirk Kerkorian, whose offer made both employees and management exceptionally nervous[21]. Whatever the reason for a hurried deal, it's clear that nobody paid attention to people, leadership, and culture issues during due diligence before signing the agreement.

The takeover was swift, as top Chrysler executives fled almost immediately[22], a problem that could have been avoided by performing proper leadership diligence and mitigating the losses with appropriate retention packages.

Cultural differences emerged immediately. Daimler's conservatism and German national culture influenced nearly every aspect of the combined enterprise, leaving American employees unable to implement the lofty plan to expand Daimler's factory capabilities and distribution network. One dark joke asked: How do you pronounce Daimler Chrysler? The answer: It's Daimler, the Chrysler is silent[23].

In 2007, Daimler sold 80% of the company to a private equity firm for $6 billion, a loss of over $20 billion in value over less than ten years.

America Online and Time Warner

No litany of epic M&A failures is complete without discussing what is widely regarded as the worst M&A deal in history, the combination of America Online and Time Warner that resulted in $99 billion in write-downs and a $200 billion decrease in stock value[24].

This tale of woe began in January of 2001 when AOL purchased Time Warner for $164 billion. For the record, most analysts believe AOL stock was already overvalued at the time. This issue became even more apparent when the dot-com bubble burst in September of 2001, but the problems ran deeper than overvaluation. The merger was supposed to combine AOL's desire to gain access to Time Warner's cable network, making it possible to deliver both the Internet and Time Warner's content to the millions of customers who would be touched by their combined presence.

On paper, the merger was a good idea, but within months AOL was losing subscribers to up-and-coming broadband providers. AOL Time Warner should have been large enough to withstand the hit and had the resources to compete in a broadband world. Not surprisingly, some reports indicate that due diligence took only a weekend to complete[25], with little thought given to the people, leadership, and culture issues that ultimately made it impossible for the company to recover from the bubble burst and shift to broadband.

According to Steve Case, AOL's CEO at the time, mistrust prevailed between the more traditional Time Warner team that thought AOL executives were arrogant, with holier-than-though attitudes[26]. The AOL team thought Time Warner executives were too conservative to catch up[27]. Time Warner itself was a mashup of disparate divisions leftover from the mergers of Time Inc. and Warner Communications, leaving small fiefdoms to resist every move the invading AOL armies made[28].

The merger also suffered from a dramatic change to the incentive plan. Time Warner provided cash incentives to managers based on their unit's performance. The combined enterprise wanted a program that would give a sense of unity and motivate employees to work for the common good, so they used company stock instead[29]. However, falling stock prices after the merger left Time Warner executives resentful of AOL, which they saw as dragging the company down and taking money out of their pockets.

The firm dropped the AOL name in 2003, just two years after the acquisition. Time Warner finally spun off AOL in 2009 with a value of about $3.5 billion[30], a loss of over $200 billion from their worth before the merger.

Why Due Diligence Matters

It's easy to dismiss these billions of dollars in losses as a cost of doing business but doing so diminishes the real effect these deals had on the world. Because these deals went so poorly, thousands of people lost their jobs, billions of dollars in retirement savings were decimated, hundreds of communities had to deal with economic uncertainty, and taxpayers had to pick up the tab through bailouts and social safety programs like unemployment insurance, nutrition funding, and cash assistance.

While we cannot say for a certainty that better due diligence and integration of people, leadership, and culture would have saved these companies, their shareholders, employees, and communities from the pain caused by these losses, firms should at least take a look at these factors when deciding whether or not a deal makes sense. Nobody is better positioned to perform this analysis than a seasoned HR practitioner.

Part 2: The Information Ecosystem

While due diligence conjures images of checklists and interviews, the savvy HR practitioner will leverage other parts of the information ecosystem to learn about the target company before they request documents and schedule interviews. The next several chapters outline the most fundamental ways an HR practitioner can get to know the target company's financial, cultural, and leadership makeup to make better decisions throughout the M&A process.

As discussed in Chapter 1, due diligence happens in stages. Practitioners have access to different pieces of information at different points in time.

The goal of the target screening phase is to make a yes or no decision on the deal. The HR practitioner will generally have access to public information and a few seller-provided documents. HR's job will be to identify any deal killers. If HR has input for the financial model or specific executive retention recommendations, it should provide that information to the business sponsor and corporate development so it can be considered prior to extending the LOI.

Once the LOI is signed, the formal due diligence phase begins. HR will have more access to seller-provided documents and may also conduct interviews and site visits. This is another opportunity to look for deal killers, give feedback on the financial model, and think about retention of critical employees. This is the point when the HR practitioner can request any changes to be made to the definitive agreement. Finally, HR will use due diligence to start planning for their role in helping the business realize the synergies that were included in the financial model.

Buying A House

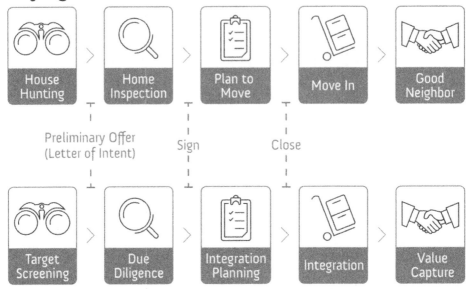

Buying A Company

After the definitive agreement is signed, the buyer has more access to the seller and integration planning starts. Business sponsors and corporate development start to make solid plans for bringing the companies together, and HR practitioners start to think about which members of the target company team should be given incentives to stay and help make sure the deal strategy is realized. HR practitioners also evaluate how they can help make the merger successful.

The company will not be able to execute integration plans until the deal is closed, at which point HR practitioners will shift from managing risks to managing change and the integration project plan.

Chapter 4: Independent Research

As soon as an HR practitioner becomes aware of a potential target company, they should begin compiling a research file. This research file should include the places the HR practitioner has gone to find information (like websites, publications, analyst reports, or Glassdoor), anything interesting they saw, their summary and analysis of that information, and questions they would like answered based on their evaluation. Conducting this research will help HR practitioners shape their thoughts about the target company, and their initial review will help ensure the later document requests and interviews are an efficient use of everybody's time.

While in these early stages, HR practitioners will almost certainly have confidentiality obligations, even if they haven't signed a formal non-disclosure agreement. Therefore, the initial research file is likely to be limited to an analysis of publicly available information.

Public Information

Most people wouldn't buy a house without first getting more information on the home and neighborhood. In addition to what the realtor provides, house hunters will spend hours combing through websites showing available properties, they'll look at maps to see how far it is from their jobs and favorite shopping places, check out the school district and crime statistics, and evaluate the cost of taxes and utilities to make sure they can afford the home. Homeowners conduct this analysis before they even set foot inside the house or talk to the seller.

Buying a company is no different, and the HR practitioner will want to start reviewing publicly available information about the target company's people, leadership, and culture.

The Target Company Website

Visits to the target company's website are a logical first step. Checking out the site may need to be coordinated with the corporate development team, as multiple visits from the acquiring company's IP address could tip off the target's IT department about the transaction.

The best place to start on the website is the "about us" section, which includes information about the company's background, mission, vision, and leadership. These pages can contain important clues about the organization's core competencies, key leaders, and culture. The company's careers page may also include a wealth of information, including their current talent needs and the employee value proposition. Some companies showcase their press releases and links to positive news stories on their webpage as well, and public companies usually host regulatory filings and annual reports on their webpage. All of these artifacts can tell us about people, leadership, and culture in the target company.

Social and Traditional Media

Reviewing the company's official Facebook, Twitter, Instagram, LinkedIn, and other social media feeds can tell HR practitioners a lot about how the organization would like to be seen by the public. This content is, of course, colored by the positive bias every organization has about itself, making it critical to see what others are saying about the organization in those same feeds by searching for mentions or hashtags.

Customer review sites like Yelp can give information about how effectively employees deal with the public and may provide insight into possible service gaps that may not be uncovered by looking at the firm's official feeds. Glassdoor reviews can provide similar insight into the employee and job seeker experience. It's not uncommon for there to be a significant disconnect between how company leadership sees itself and how the employees perceive leadership.

More formal sources of information include news stories about the target company and its key leaders. Sometimes a simple Google search will turn up scads of data. Other times, it pays to look at more sophisticated research tools like LexisNexis. Analyst reports, Dun & Bradstreet profiles, or other niche industry sources may also be helpful.

Finally, some organizations choose to look at court filings related to the target. When made public, lawsuits can help expose potential problems in a target company's handling of sensitive issues.

In-House Experts

One often overlooked source of information on the target company is the acquiring company's employee base. If the target company is a competitor, a member of the strategy team may have compiled a dossier that covers the target's primary capabilities and critical employees, alongside some cultural clues. Some of the acquiring company's employees may have worked for the other firm and could also provide insight into the target company's people, leadership, and culture. The target may be a vendor to the acquirer, in which case somebody may want to chat with the supplier management team member responsible for the relationship. Similarly, if the company is a customer, the acquirer's sales team could have a wealth of competitive information.

The confidential nature of the transaction makes requesting this information tricky, so it may be prudent to have in-house experts sign a non-disclosure agreement. If that's not feasible, a discussion about the industry in general and then a narrower focus onto not just the target but other similar companies may be a way to ensure the employee doesn't provide information that's subject to confidentiality obligations or gain knowledge that might be misused. Before engaging in this type of information gathering, make sure to contact the company legal department or an attorney who can guide the plan.

Competitive Intelligence and Outside Experts

On occasion, a buyer may request the services of an outside firm to assist in due diligence. These external firms specialize in digging up information on the target company, which may be helpful when the target company is unaware of the potential bid or when it would be awkward for the buyer to request sensitive information.

While many organizations do some level of competitive intelligence in-house, securing an outside partner may result in a less biased view of the target company. The service will compile a report that delves into the target's business plans, markets, major customers, sales funnels, expansion plans, and other critical facets of the business. Credible competitive intelligence firms abide by a code of conduct, and use ethical means to source information, avoiding the appearance of illegal industrial espionage.

Organizational benchmarking is one subset of competitive intelligence. It allows the buyer to map the target company's critical organizations as part of the due diligence process, essentially creating organizational charts and key employee profiles with a detailed list of employees, their titles, locations, and reporting relationships. Some competitive intelligence firms will compile profiles of key employees and may even be able to assess their risk of flight in the case of a merger or acquisition.

Outside experts may also include private investigators, computer experts, or other researchers to probe financial transactions, determine asset ownership, uncover intellectual property issues, or explore cybersecurity weaknesses. Retaining outside experts can be tricky and can even be creepy if the experts violate personal privacy norms. The business leader engaging the outside expert should consult with legal counsel to ensure compliance with privacy laws and general business ethics.

Chapter 5: Information from the Seller

In addition to independent research, HR practitioners will most likely have the opportunity to gather additional information from the seller. This information can come in a variety of forms, including presentations, documents, spreadsheets, and interviews. Information provided by the seller should also be kept in the target company research file, as it will be necessary for the final risk analysis.

The Confidential Information Memorandum

When a person is ready to sell their home, their realtor will create a listing that provides basic information about the property. The listing includes the selling price, annual taxes, size of the home and the lot, the school district, recent remodeling, and other unique selling features. There are usually a ton of pictures of the home's exterior alongside stunning photos of a well-staged interior. The narrative tells the buyer about the beautiful views, charming neighborhood, and access to the freeway. The listing gets the buyer interested in checking out the house.

In an M&A transaction, the confidential information memorandum, usually referred to as a CIM (pronounced sim), replaces the listing. The CIM is generally drafted by a banker or advisor who will collect a commission or fee when the business sells, though some firms create the CIM in-house. Like a real estate listing, it is designed to get business sponsors and corporate development teams interested in checking out the company. However, the CIM usually doesn't include a purchase price, leaving an initial valuation up to the buyer.

The CIM usually opens with an executive summary that relays the value proposition of the acquisition to the potential buyer. This is followed by a brief company history, founder biographies, and information on the purpose of the firm. The next section speaks to the company's core capabilities, including general information on how products and services are developed, manufactured or created, delivered or distributed, and sold to customers.

The next part features a summary of the industry and market opportunities, including opportunities for growth. The CIM often uses this section to highlight proprietary processes, intellectual property, critical resources, and leadership team capabilities, as the company will leverage these capabilities to exploit growth opportunities. This section may also include information on the workforce, such as headcount, critical skills, locations, and functional breakouts.

The last portion contains several years of high-level financial information, including historical data and detailed future projections. The financials will occasionally include workforce costs.

There are situations where the target company will not create a CIM. Sometimes the target company is too small to justify the expense. The target company may only be talking to one or two firms they already know. Other times, the buyer may be initiating the process, making a CIM unnecessary. Finally, the target company may not be for sale at all, which may happen in the case of a hostile takeover.

The CIM is useful for gaining a baseline understanding of how the target company sees itself and its core capabilities. By the time an HR practitioner has reviewed the CIM and completed their initial research, they may have compiled an initial set of questions about the target company. These questions should become part of the research file, and asked while gathering more information during formal due diligence.

Seller-Provided Documents

More experienced sellers, or those sellers working with seasoned advisors, will provide many documents upfront, including financial statements, regulatory filings, board resolutions, employment agreements, compensation plans, and equity information (often in the form of a capitalization table, which we will discuss later). HR practitioners should at least peruse all of these documents as they tend to include details about key leaders and the workforce.

Because M&A transactions require a great deal of confidentiality, the seller or their advisor typically creates a secure document repository, known as a virtual data room or VDR. The VDR allows the seller to upload sensitive documents to a safe cloud storage space. The seller will generally organize the VDR into several sections, including a folder for

HR documents. Sellers and their advisors often scatter HR data throughout the VDR, so HR practitioners should review each folder, paying particular mind to the legal and financial folders.

The screen capture below shows a typical folder structure inside a VDR (in this case, DealRoom). An HR practitioner is likely to find information on people, leadership, and culture in nearly every folder of this VDR.

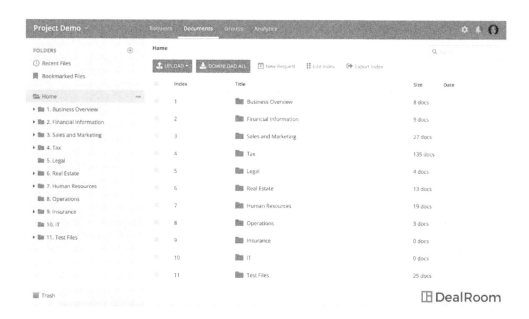

The Checklist and Additional Document Requests

Chances are good the information provided in the data room will not be sufficient to answer all of the relevant questions, so the HR practitioner will need to ask for additional documents. Many buyers use a checklist to ask the seller to place additional information in the VDR.

There are hundreds of M&A checklists available on the Internet, but HR M&A experts created very few of them. Instead, these checklists were put together by finance and investment professionals who are primarily interested in financial, operational, and compliance risks. HR practitioners also need to concern themselves with leadership, culture, and HR functional risks to fully support the integration plan and help create deal value. The HR M&A Roundtable has created a suggested checklist that includes these items and can be downloaded from our website at www.MandARoundtable.com.

Checklist Etiquette

One of the major errors new HR practitioners make is sending an entire unedited checklist to the seller. Even the best list can only be a starting point for information requests. Because every deal is different, the checklist should be customized to meet the needs of the specific industry, target company, and integration plan. Customizing the request doesn't only mean that items will be added; it's just as likely that a few will need to be removed as well.

Not only is sending an unedited checklist inefficient, but it can be overwhelming for both sides. Without an edited checklist, the HR practitioner of the acquiring company can end up looking at documents they don't care about or drive the seller crazy, answering the same question two or three times. For example, if the buyer has been asked to provide their employee handbook and then asked separate questions about at-will employment, paid time off, and progressive discipline, that may be a waste of everybody's time when all of that information could have been gotten directly from the handbook.

Multiple functions asking the same question in different ways can also be frustrating to a seller. The buyer looks disorganized when both HR and finance are asking about benefits costs, and HR and legal each request copies of employment contracts. Evaluate the requests made by other groups and adjust the checklist accordingly.

The better practice is for the HR practitioner to create a list of questions they need to have answered. The first round of target-provided documents can be used to help identify and fill in the blanks. Then, if the seller hasn't already addressed a particular issue, additional records can be requested or any remaining questions can be asked as part of the due diligence interview.

Remember, the due diligence process also provides an opportunity for the seller to learn about the buyer. Building collegial relationships at this point in the process will be necessary if the transaction closes and the buyer and seller work together through integration and beyond.

Due Diligence Interviews and Site Visits

Around the same time as document requests are being made, the target company's leaders will be interviewed about their HR practices. The acquiring company will likely hold separate calls for each functional area, including discussions about finances, products, legal matters, and other vital issues. If the target company has an HR team, there is usually an opportunity for a practitioner-to-practitioner discussion at this point. Some sellers will provide a presentation before the due diligence interview, but don't depend on one being available.

Due diligence interviews allow HR practitioners to ask questions that can't be answered efficiently in emails between the parties. These interviews usually last one to two hours and contain a walkthrough of the target's talent philosophy, key leaders and employees, organizational structure, total rewards practices, performance management approach, labor and employee relations issues, company culture, and HR service delivery. Depending on the topic's sensitivity and meeting attendees, some questions might be pulled into separate interviews.

Depending on the acquiring organization's budget and norms, the due diligence interviews may be either over the phone or face-to-face. Face-to-face meetings are preferable as they provide the opportunity to perform a site visit. Going onsite affords the HR practitioner a chance to see the physical space and learn how the team interacts. Site visits are usually incognito, so wearing a company badge or a shirt with the company logo is a bad idea. Remember, nobody is supposed to know about the deal yet, so visitors from the acquiring company should dress to blend in.

Interview Etiquette

Whether a due diligence interview is virtual or in-person, practitioners want to go in well-prepared. Read the documents the target has already provided. Review all of the research notes compiled to date. Have questions ready. Be sure to coordinate with the corporate development team so expectations are clear. Likewise, HR practitioners should communicate their concerns so other team members can listen to the answers and look for other clues that will help make the most of the acquirer's time with the target company.

Keep in mind that this is probably the first contact the target company will have with the HR practitioner. It pays to be friendly! Remember, it's an interview and not an interrogation. The target is evaluating the buyer just as much as the acquirer is evaluating the seller. The formal due diligence phase is almost universally seen as the lowest point in the deal lifecycle since it feels like an inquisition where the buyer pressures the seller to answer question after question. HR practitioners can make it a little easier by being prepared and professional.

Working with Limited Information

Even with a thorough checklists and well-developed interview agenda, HR practitioners are not likely to obtain every piece of information they need to feel completely comfortable proceeding with a transaction. Sellers can become overwhelmed by multiple requests and must prioritize their responses, which often means replies to HR play second fiddle to financial and legal matters. They may not have the information readily available or the team members responsible for gathering the data may not be aware of the transaction. Whatever the reason, HR practitioners should not expect to get everything they want—or need—from the seller.

HR practitioners are left with two choices when information is missing. First, they can record the missing data as a potential risk, using the model shared in Chapter 14. The second option is to work with the business sponsor and corporate development, explaining why the information is required to move forward with the deal. Stalling a transaction over missing information will require a strong business case, meaning there must be a significant financial, operational, or compliance reason to slow things down.

M&A is inherently risky and successfully navigating the process will require the ability to operate in an ambiguous environment. When data is missing, HR practitioners will need to apply a high degree of professional judgment to determine how they move forward.

Chapter 6: HR Topics

While the current state of M&A largely downplays the importance of people, leadership, and culture factors, the landscape is changing. The trend toward recognizing people as a critical contributor to business success is not limited to M&A. In 2019, both the United States Securities and Exchange Commission (SEC)[1] and the International Standards Organization (ISO)[2] took steps toward formalizing how businesses should think about their human capital. The ISO committee specifically considered M&A when developing their human capital reporting standard[3].

The list of topics in this chapter combines years of M&A experience with the guidance these organizations provide to help HR practitioners think holistically about the role of people in both the target company and the future combined organization. This section is organized in rough order of importance to finance and strategy stakeholders to help HR practitioners prioritize the limited time they'll have to conduct due diligence. HR practitioners will need to customize this list to meet the needs of their organizations and deals.

Executive Information

The first item most corporate development teams request is information on current and recently separated key employees, officers, and directors. They will look for bios, resumes, employment agreements or similar contracts, and resignation letters along with separation agreements and releases. The HR practitioner will also want to be aware of any executive, officer, or director who has been accused of a crime or is subject to civil litigation.

Business sponsors and corporate development team members use these to help decide if the leadership team has the potential to be capable partners in combining the firms. If the prospects are good, they then use these documents to screen for significant legal, financial, and intellectual property risks. This information is critical to retention planning during target screening, formal due diligence, and integration planning.

Headcount and Pay Data

The most foundational HR documents the seller provides are an organization chart and employee census file. The level of detail will usually depend on the deal size and seller sophistication. It is not uncommon for the org charts to be anonymized, showing only the employee's department, location, and title.

The employee census file is a spreadsheet with the details of each employee and contractor in the organization. Each employee entry should include a unique identifier (possibly the employee name), date of hire, job title, job code, and position. Some sellers will include a brief job description or employee biographical information such as skill level, unique capabilities, or education level in the file. Other information may consist of function, product line, union membership, and location. For complicated or international deals, the employing entity also needs to be provided.

It shouldn't be a surprise if the seller is unwilling to provide certain employee information, like employees' names or other personally sensitive data (such as date of birth, age, race, gender, ethnicity, nationality, immigration status, or union membership) at the start of the formal due diligence phase. The patchwork of international privacy laws has sellers concerned about the significant fines associated with violating an employee's right to privacy. If there are concerns about safely handling employee data, consult with an attorney or privacy expert.

Finally, the file should contain employee type and status, including whether an employee is full-time, part-time, seasonal, temporary, a migrant worker, or contractor. The list should also include employees who are on leave, sabbatical, or furlough to provide a complete picture.

When evaluating employee status, be sure to discuss any third-party labor the target company uses. Gather information on contractor arrangements and any steps the target takes to ensure that contractors are appropriately classified and are not employees as less sophisticated organizations frequently misclassify de facto employees as contractors.

It's also surprisingly common to find a target company that doesn't have consolidated contractor information available during the early due diligence stages. One HR M&A Roundtable member reported finding out the target company had over 40 contractors in Eastern Europe when she reviewed the employee schedules in the final contract; the seller hadn't mentioned the contractors at any prior point.

Total Rewards

In most cases, the corporate development team will request the information required to calculate the cost of compensation and benefits so they can include it in the financial model for the deal. While this information is helpful, it may not be sufficient to allow HR practitioners to complete a total rewards side-by-side. The side-by-side is a tool HR practitioner use to compare the acquired employee's current total rewards picture against what they will experience after integration. A basic side-by-side template appears in Chapter 8.

Completing the side-by-side analysis is probably not enough to fully understand the target company's total rewards picture. Between HR interviews and independent research on sites like Glassdoor, HR practitioners should have a sense of whether employees are satisfied with their pay and benefits or have a particular attachment to a workplace perk. The amount of angst caused by changing something as simple as paid parking or gym memberships is surprising, and HR practitioners who know the complete picture are more likely to successfully navigate the minefield of total rewards change.

Compensation and Equity

The seller should include detailed pay information with the employee census file. The census file should detail pay elements, including base pay as either an hourly or salaried rate, depending on how they compensate the employee. Furthermore, short-term incentive programs like bonuses, commissions, profit- or gain-sharing should be disclosed. Long-term incentive information may appear in either the employee census file or capitalization table. HR practitioners should also find out about any outstanding employee loans.

Several years of detailed bonus information may be required to analyze employee compensation accurately. Details should include bonus targets and actual attainment. Where possible, securing copies of the written bonus plans and offer letters can make this analysis far more manageable. Request overtime information from employers with large hourly employee populations, including an average number of weekly hours worked by non-exempt employees. Finally, determine what monetary rewards and recognition programs the target uses to motivate and retain employees, as they may be a significant part of an employee's pay.

Along with cash compensation data, the buyer should receive a capitalization table (frequently called the cap table). The cap table provides information on every person or entity who has equity in the company, including employees, advisors, and investors, among others. The cap table is discussed in more detail in Chapter 18. In addition to the cap table, buyers often request written information on equity, including granting plans, option plans, employee stock purchase plans, and the like. Many buyers also request copies of board resolutions approving each grant to ensure they're in good order.

Some acquirers find it valuable to request executive compensation plans separately. Executive total rewards may be significantly different than what most employees earn, with distinct equity and bonus structures alongside a different set of perquisites. Some key employees may have arrangements related to the sale of the target company, including transaction bonuses tied to the sale of the business, cash retention plans, accelerated equity vesting, enhanced severances, and other kinds of golden parachutes or deferred compensation plans. Sometimes special arrangements extend to non-employees, including officers, directors, and advisors.

During the due diligence interview, HR practitioners can ask about the target's compensation philosophy, assuming they're mature enough to have one. This request should include the benchmarking approach, job architecture, pay structures, and compensation procedures. It can also be helpful to evaluate the target company's job descriptions and salary schedules.

Awareness of the target company's pay mix and incentive plans is critical, especially if employees will experience any changes as a result of the integration. Short of laying people off, society sees changing an employee's pay structure as one of the most malevolent actions a company can take.

Benefits and Perquisites

This section is presented from the perspective of an HR practitioner in the United States. If any party to the transaction is located outside the US, similar documentation will be needed, but it may go by a different name. The same is true of the compliance items covered later in this chapter. If the HR practitioner isn't familiar with international labor law in jurisdictions affected by the transaction—including employee transfer or redundancy legislation—they should secure the services of a professional to avoid compliance issues.

Health, Welfare, and Retirement Plans

Most due diligence checklists include requests for medical, dental, and vision insurance plan documents, alongside retiree medical, and both defined benefit and defined contribution retirement plans. The requested materials usually cover the most urgent cost and compliance information but may not be sufficient for a thorough HR practitioner analysis.

Finance professionals want to make sure they understand the cost structure and financing of the plan by looking at cost schedules, actuarial and trust accounting reports, and financial statements detailing administrative costs, employee loans, contributions, and distributions. In the US, these professionals review summary plan descriptions (SDPs) and COBRA compliance data alongside correspondence with the Internal Revenue Service (IRS) or Pension Benefit Guaranty Corporation (PBGC) or similar agencies to ensure that all plans comply with the Employee Retirement Income Security Act (ERISA) and other applicable law. Find out if the company participates in any multi-employer plans. Most employee loans are from the company's 401(k) plan, but some employers will make direct loans to employees.

To complete the health and welfare side-by-side, HR practitioners need information on the employee cost of health insurance, especially premiums, deductibles, and out of pocket maximums. Company-paid contributions to high-deductible health plans and health reimbursement arrangements will also dramatically shape the employee benefits picture beyond the financial information corporate development teams usually request. Finally, consider the costs of wellness programs like health assessments and coaching programs.

Time Off Programs

Paid time off programs typically include holidays, sick time, and vacations. Some companies also offer various forms of paid and unpaid leave, including sabbaticals. Parental and military leave plans are also standard and may go beyond statutory minimums. The HR practitioner will need to know if there are any employees on various leaves and when they are expected to return to work.

In addition to possibly moving employees to new time off programs, time off plans should be reviewed for historical compliance, especially as new laws governing time off continue to emerge around the United States. Depending on how employees transfer, accrued employee entitlements, like earned but unpaid sick and vacation time, could be material to the transaction.

Severance

Depending on the final acquisition workforce plan, modeling and managing severance costs may be significant. When this is the case, HR practitioners should partner with finance professionals and other experts to understand the impact of severance decisions. Factors that HR practitioners must consider are company policy, individual employee agreements, collective bargaining provisions, and local law.

In addition to the financial impacts of severance, how an acquirer chooses to exit employees will affect morale and productivity for employees who "survive" downsizing efforts. The HR practitioner will need to consider this as the integration plan is developed.

Perquisites

For the purposes of this book, a perk is a privilege or gain employees experience as a result of their work. Perks can include a variety of direct financial incentives, like uniform allowances, paid parking, bus passes, meals, gym memberships, and company cars. Convenience benefits like onsite daycare, massages, company stores, and dry cleaning, which the employee has to pay for, can also be considered perks. Other perks might come from the work environment and can include flexible work schedules, telecommuting, healthy snack options, an onsite gym, or the infamous start-up ping pong table.

Many employees view their office traditions as perks. Rituals like employee recognition programs, doughnut Fridays, and how the company celebrates birthdays or retirements may be meaningful to the employee experience.

The list of potential perks is limitless, but employees notice when perks go away. HR practitioners should strive to understand the perks at all key locations—not just the target's headquarters—and have a plan for transitioning them. Perks often seem like a small issue, but tales of employee revolts due to the removal of formal tea service and free soda abound.

Workforce Strategies

Awareness of the target company's current headcount is a good start, but HR practitioners need to have a handle on the organization's past and future. Furthermore, HR practitioners should understand the overarching strategies and goals the company has in place for its workforce. Strategy evaluation includes understanding the target's most significant concerns about the workforce and how they plan to address them. This may encompass several HR matters, including attracting and retaining talent, developing the workforce, and managing costs. It can also be helpful to understand what management is measuring, which might include things like worker productivity, internal promotions, time spent in training, safety incidents, or lost time. This information is helpful to conduct a thorough formal due diligence and is necessary for integration planning, especially when there are talent-related synergies in the financial model.

Workforce Planning

Sellers occasionally restructure their workforce to make the company more attractive to potential buyers, resulting in a team that is unable to meet future revenue projections or is on the verge of burnout. Looking at voluntary and involuntary turnover trends, including reasons for past attrition, can help the HR practitioner partner with other business leaders to see if a material change in the number of employees will be required to meet the investment thesis.

If the workforce is likely to increase, understanding how the target and acquirer will work together to meet hiring needs is critical. Depending on who will be responsible for hiring, HR practitioners will need insight into recruitment and hiring practices, onboarding methods, cost per hire metrics, the average time to fill, outside agency utilization, and other factors relevant to sustaining the future business. HR practitioners should also evaluate any pending offers as there may be outstanding offers that have not yet been accepted, or offers that have been accepted but the person has not yet started.

If a material change will be the result of a headcount decrease, the HR practitioner will need to evaluate severance costs and timing. Likewise, if there are planned terminations, with or without cause, individually or collectively, HR will want to know about them along with any associated releases and waivers that are requested from exiting employees. Depending on the size and age of the workforce, likely retirements should also be considered, along with projected early retirements because of the merger. Recent reductions in force should also be reviewed, including compliance with the Worker Adjustment and Retraining Notification Act (WARN) and similar laws.

Performance Management Systems

Understanding the target's performance management systems can provide insights into how the organization manages its workforce. Is performance management mandatory? What is the performance management cycle? Do they use a forced distribution ranking system? Is performance linked to pay or promotions? Is performance linked to development? These questions can help the HR practitioner get a better picture of the target's practices and provide valuable clues about their culture.

HR practitioners may also want to gather information on the company's disciplinary practices. How do they manage absenteeism or poor performance? Do they consistently apply a progressive discipline approach? Is an appeals process or alternative dispute resolution available? What about a union grievance process? If any employees are currently suspended or at risk of termination, HR may need to gather details on the situation.

Career Development and Training

A final category for HR practitioners to consider is career development, which is becoming an increasingly important part of the employer value proposition. Employee development goes beyond mandatory training topics, time, and costs and should include both formal and informal development opportunities.

HR practitioners can use the due diligence process to ascertain whether the target ties learning opportunities to career paths or ladders, leadership skills development programs, or succession planning. Does the target have a formal high potential leadership program? Do they have formal programs, like tuition reimbursement and paid conference attendance, which can be meaningful for maintaining employee skills and morale? Do they pay for certification classes, tests, or continuing education units to maintain credentials? Are there informal programs, including learning service subscriptions and time off for networking events, which can motivate employees to get better at their jobs and may aid retention and culture-building?

Compliance Matters

Handbooks, Policies, and Procedures

During the formal due diligence phase, the target company will usually provide the employee handbook along with any policies and procedures that affect the acquired workforce. When possible, review these documents before the interview. Even a brief flip through the pages may allow HR practitioners to ask better questions that are likely to result in additional insight into other due diligence areas.

Standard policies that are not mentioned in other parts of this chapter include the code of ethics or code of conduct, background checks, media relations or outside communications, and acceptable use of company equipment.

Offer Letters and Agreements

The HR practitioner should receive copies of all standard forms used as employee applications, employment offers, or other employment agreements. Additionally, they'll want to review any employment arrangements that do not conform to the standards. Some employees may have verbal or "handshake" agreements, which need to be understood as well.

Copies of confidentiality, non-compete, non-solicitation, intellectual property, and other agreements employees are required to sign should be secured. It's also up to the HR practitioner to ensure that all employees demonstrate the legal right to work in a jurisdiction, such as completing an I-9 form.

Litigation, Claims, and Audits

The corporate development team will usually request information on past, potential, and active claims, charges, audits, litigation, and settlement agreements related to a list of compliance matters. These can include workers' compensation, unemployment, immigration, termination, and wage and hour matters, among others.

Harassment and discrimination matters will also require review, including sexual harassment and discrimination based on race, age, disability, leave, or other factors. Whistleblower and retaliation claims should also be reviewed. Any notices from the Department of Labor, EEOC, OFCCP, or similar local, state, or federal agencies should be provided to the buyer along with reports and documents submitted to these agencies (including affirmative action plans, EEO-1s, and VETS 100s).

Workplace Health and Safety

Health and safety issues can be significant. Proper due diligence begins with requesting any OSHA or similar paperwork the target maintains. In the absence of these reports, gather information on safety training, workers' compensation claims, lost time, accidents, or deaths.

Collective Bargaining

Finally, if the target company has a union or works council, or has knowledge of organizing activities, the HR practitioner should obtain copies of all relevant documents, including contracts, collective bargaining agreements, and the like. They'll also need information on ongoing or possible negotiations as well as strikes, stoppages, or slowdowns in addition to any claims of an unfair labor practice or other violation.

Culture and Engagement

At its heart, culture is about how things get done inside an organization. The phases between target assessment and integration planning provide HR practitioners the opportunity to learn how the target company does things, and how difficult it will be for the employees to change their behaviors and practices during integration. The company's website will provide insight into the employee value proposition and may share information on important rituals that can help the HR practitioner learn what's important to the target. The company website can also tell the acquiring team what the company values based on their involvement in the community.

The handbook and policies will show what behaviors the company wants to reinforce, the business tools will help the HR practitioner understand how information flows, and workforce planning and employee development practices can provide insight into which skills and characteristics the company wants to build. Compensation and performance management programs show whether the company rewards individual performance or is more egalitarian in its approach.

Both employee engagement surveys and information on Glassdoor will share employees' perceptions of leadership and communication styles, work-life balance, and total rewards. Be mindful that these anonymous forums can create a more cynical view, as it is often the most disaffected employees who will take the time to share their thoughts.

The HR practitioner should check their assumptions during the due diligence interview by asking direct questions about the company's values and which ones are most prized in the organization. What happens when people violate those values? The company's preferred leadership style and how decisions are made in the organization should also be discussed. Finally, HR needs to know how the target company handles internal communications, which will be necessary for building an effective change management plan.

When possible, a site visit provides additional information about the organization's culture. It also allows the HR practitioner to "gut check" information provided by the target and its employees. If the organization says morale is high, but the employees seem melancholy, it's probably worth exploring. The site visit is also an opportunity to look at the physical space, which can reveal information about hierarchies and the key messages the target company wants every employee to see when they come to work.

The HR practitioner needs to be mindful of cultural bubbles that exist in many organizations. The environment in a rural Pennsylvania manufacturing plant will probably be different from the environment and interactions that occur in the Atlanta headquarters. This same dynamic can occur during interviews, where a leader who sits at HQ attempts to represent an entire global organization.

HR Service Delivery

The target company's HR service delivery model is the final area to evaluate. The acquiring company needs to find out if HR is represented on the target company's leadership team and is part of critical business decisions. This includes gathering information on HR's reputation and understanding the budget for the HR function. The acquiring company's HR team should ask about the company's current HR organization and how they handle HR duties, including which HR systems and tools they use. Understanding how HR services will be delivered in the combined organization is critical to helping achieve any deal synergies related to people.

Chapter 7: The Post-Diligence Huddle

When a buyer is mature enough to engage HR practitioners in the formal due diligence phase, they are usually engaging experts from multiple departments. Each function is requesting documents and meetings with the target company, asking different questions, and bringing different perspectives to the due diligence process. Sadly, most acquirers ignore the collective wisdom of the team when completing their due diligence process.

After the due diligence interviews and site visits are over, either HR practitioners or the IMO should initiate a post-diligence huddle. (As I noted in the introduction, I borrowed this practice from an HR M&A Roundtable member on one of the first deals I led, and I've continued to use it to great success.) HR practitioners are strongly encouraged to harness the wisdom of the crowd, even if it means calling other due diligence leads for a one-on-one discussion should the huddle be impractical for their organization.

The first question for HR practitioners to ask during the post-diligence huddle is "how will we either break or enhance the target company's business when we move employees away from their current ways of doing things and toward the end state?" Part of well-executed due diligence is determining what processes and practices might break as a result of the integration, and where there's room to improve. Depending on the nature of any proposed synergies, follow-on questions related to specific synergies may be appropriate.

This initial question is designed to get at culture but frames it in a way that other business leaders will understand. Many organizations don't appreciate the word "culture." Substitute phrases like "operational readiness" or "integration challenges" can be used to bridge the gap. This approach has the added benefit of providing a cross-functional view of culture. This information will become part of the integration plan, which will be discussed in Chapter 17.

The second question HR practitioners should ask is "who are the key people we should retain?" This question should also be broken into several follow-on items addressing who is required to lead through the integration process, and which people are critical to the long-term

71

success of the business. Asking this question helps HR practitioners get a head start on the retention planning process, which is discussed in Chapter 18.

At the end of this process, the HR practitioner will compile a formal due diligence report, which is discussed further in Chapter 20.

Part 3: Identifying and Assessing HR Risks

N ow that we've set the context for the due diligence process, it's worth reiterating our definition of due diligence.

Due diligence is the art and science of identifying, assessing, and mitigating risks associated with an M&A transaction.

The human capital risks associated with an M&A transaction are limitless, and an enthusiastic HR practitioner may want to capture every risk related to running a firm with employees. This approach is not likely to be successful, given the short timelines associated with the due diligence process. Formal due diligence periods as short as one week are not uncommon, and many HR practitioners have told me they feel lucky to get a "long" due diligence period of three weeks.

Making the most of this accelerated timeline requires extreme focus on those items that are most likely to create material issues after the transaction closes. Human capital professionals can sort these risks into six distinct areas: financial, operational, compliance, leadership, culture, and HR functional, each of which is defined below.

Financial Risk	Any risk that may have a direct material impact on the organization's balance sheet or the transaction's economic model.
Operational Risk	Any risk that has a direct impact on the organization's ability to deliver products and services to customers.
Compliance Risk	Any risk that may lead to government-imposed fines or penalties and would likely harm the organization's reputation.
Leadership Risk	Any risk that may cause the organization to lack clear direction during or after the M&A event.
Culture Risk	Any risk that changing processes will harm the organization's ability to deliver products and services to customers.
HR Functional Risk	Any risk that impacts HR's ability to deliver services to employees and leaders.

The items most business leaders would consider more important appear at the top of this list. For example, the CFO is less likely to be concerned about the lack of a succession plan for one of the C-suite leaders (leadership risk) than a potential back pay liability of $100,000 (financial risk). The list should help the HR practitioner prioritize the limited time they have to help the business leaders make critical decisions on a deal.

The cold reality of M&A is that finance professionals, bankers, and advisors drive most due diligence processes, limiting their focus to the financial and legal aspects of a transaction. This approach is shortsighted, and Harvard Business Review agrees most deal makers "underestimate the significance of people issues in mergers and acquisitions."[1] We can either bemoan the fact that they would prefer to focus on spreadsheets and presentation decks, or we can accept that reality and influence the deal by speaking their language. The latter approach is more likely to be successful.

Some risks will fall into more than one category, and some risks that are important in the acquiring organization may not be reflected here at all. The HR practitioner should revise the due diligence process to reflect the organization's unique priorities and the integration strategy for the acquisition.

Chapter 8: Financial Risk

Financial risk includes any risk that may have a direct material impact on the organization's balance sheet or the transaction's economic model. There are only a few HR risks that fall into this category, but HR practitioners must recognize and raise these risks. In addition to helping shape the financial model for the transaction, being able to communicate these risks to Business sponsors and the corporate development team better positions the HR practitioner to be a trusted advisor on other deal elements.

Influencing the Financial Model

Political realities aside, the financial model for the transaction is top of mind for executives pursuing inorganic growth. The model is the subject of intense scrutiny by the firm's board or most senior leadership. Many firms use the target screening phase to evaluate public information and the CIM to decide if the financial model is viable and present an introductory offer to the seller via the LOI. Once the seller accepts the preliminary proposal, the formal due diligence phase kicks off with the primary purpose of validating and potentially adjusting the purchase price.

For an HR practitioner to influence the financial model, they must be aware of the assumptions involved. Some corporate development teams are very protective of the deal model assumptions, making it difficult for HR to add value to the process. Other groups are excited to have a financially savvy HR practitioner help ensure the model's accuracy. M&A is one of many areas where relationships matter, and HR needs to consciously build bridges with the other functions to be included and influence the deal.

Debt service is the first HR financial risk most corporate development teams evaluate. This risk typically includes defined benefit pensions or retiree medical plans. It should also include statutory retirement plans that are carried like defined benefit liabilities on the company's books. The finance team is usually aware of these liabilities early in the deal, but HR practitioners should be sure to include these issues in their analysis and report.

Changes to employee total rewards may be material to the transaction. If the average employee burden rate for the seller is significantly different from the burden rate projected for the buyer's proposed integration plan, it should be reflected in the financial model. Compiling a total rewards side-by-side will help with the burden analysis, and a sample template appears next in this chapter. The economic model should also include planned changes to the workforce, including recruiting and severance costs, as applicable.

Total Rewards Side-by-Side Analysis

The primary concern of most M&A professionals is the financial impact of the transaction, and HR practitioners earn their seat at the table by showing they understand the costs associated with the deal. Furthermore, when it's time to integrate the acquisition, employees who remain employed by the acquirer will be affected by changes to their total rewards. To help create a comprehensive picture of the total rewards cost impacts, many HR practitioners generate a total rewards side-by-side.

A total rewards side-by-side allows the HR practitioner to see how the target company's current compensation, benefits, and perks will align with the post-integration compensation, benefits, and perks. To complete this analysis, the HR practitioner must understand the integration plan. For example, if the integration plan calls for the target company to remain standalone, the side-by-side may be irrelevant. If the intention is a full integration of the acquired company, the side-by-side provides a roadmap. If the leadership team has yet to decide on an integration approach, a side-by-side analysis can allow the HR practitioner to help shape the plan by recommending a final state for the total rewards, such as pulling employees into the acquirer's health and welfare plans while leaving their incentive structures unchanged.

The HR practitioner may need to create several side-by-sides if the target company has multiple operating units with different total rewards schemes, collective bargaining agreements with specific benefits provisions, or has subsidiaries that they haven't fully integrated. Some HR practitioners choose to create additional side-by-sides when there are unusual executive pay plans.

Similarly, if an acquisition involves people outside the United States, the HR practitioner may need to create a side-by-side for each country where there is an affected employee. Many nations have strict laws governing the treatment of employee total rewards during an M&A event. Compiling the side-by-side may provide an excellent starting point for consultation with an expert on transfer legislation in each jurisdiction with employees affected by the deal.

A basic sample total rewards side-by-side template for US operations appears below. HR practitioners will need to modify this template based on the specifics of each deal. A customizable version can be found on the HR M&A Roundtable website at www.MandARoundtable.com. Only some of the items in the side-by-side analysis will be relevant to the corporate development team working on a specific acquisition. The HR practitioner will need to exercise professional judgment in how much of this information is pertinent to the corporate development team's overall deal analysis and which elements are more relevant to HR's integration planning.

Other Places to Look for Financial Impact

Other risk areas will carry financial impacts that should be reported to the business sponsor and corporate development as the HR practitioner works through the entire due diligence process. Other risk areas to be included in the due diligence report are discussed in the following chapters. Chapter 9 covers operation risks, which is where most deal synergies are realized. The cost of HR programs that support synergy realization (like the cost of training programs or new hiring) needs to be part of the financial analysis. Chapter 10 covers compliance risks where violations may require back pay and fines, for example, violations of the Fair Labor Standards Act (FLSA) and mandatory sick time accrual regulations. Chapters 11 and 12 discuss leadership and culture risks, some of which are mitigated through retention payments (discussed in detail in Chapter 18) that should be considered in the financial model. Finally, Chapter 13 discusses the HR function, which may incur additional hard costs associated with delivering services, including adding HR headcount or increased third-party outlays.

HR practitioners will want to work closely with their finance teams to find the best way to capture and report any factors that will affect the deal financial model. It's perhaps the best way for HR to earn a seat at the M&A table.

Sample Total Rewards Side-by-Side Template for US Operations

Area	Acquirer	Target	Cost Impact	Comments & Recommendations
Annual Payroll				
Base Pay				
Pay Increases				
Performance Management				
Incentive Plans				
Other Bonus Plans				
Equity Granting				
Employee Stock Purchase Plans				
Employee Stock Option Plans				
Medical Plans				
Dental Plans				
Vision Plans				
Flexible Spending Accounts				
Wellness Programs				
Employee Assistance Program				
Pensions				
Retirement Plans				
Life Insurance				
Disability Insurance				
Other Insurances				
Holidays				
Paid Time Off				
Paid and Unpaid Leaves				
Sabbatical				
Other Time Off Programs				
Company Cars				
Paid Parking				
Meals and Snacks				
Gym Memberships				
Pet Insurance				
Legal Insurance				
Financial Planning				
Work-Life Balance Perks				
Career Development Perks				
Other Perks				
Severance Plans				

Chapter 9: Operational Risk

Operational risk covers findings that have a direct impact on the organization's ability to deliver products and services to customers. These risks are often difficult to define without at least some knowledge of the final integration model, meaning most of them will be discovered during the formal due diligence and integration planning phases, after target screening is complete.

Organizational Structure

The first major operating area for HR to review is the organizational structure. Business sponsors usually perform this due diligence step with HR as a critical stakeholder. This step requires an understanding of the target company's business units, headcounts, and locations. Next, HR practitioners should understand the capabilities and goals of each business unit, including an analysis of how well the business unit is meeting their goals and how the target company's results compare with the acquirer's expectations.

HR practitioners will need to have a sense of the overall organizational reporting structure, the spans and layers involved in the organization's hierarchy, and who is empowered to make decisions. This analysis often overlaps with leadership due diligence (see Chapter 11).

Organizational information appears in several places, including the company website and CIM. Remember, the company is going to sell itself in the best possible light, so looking at the news, outside analysts, customers, and other stakeholder opinions can be helpful.

Staffing Levels

The next set of operational risks for HR practitioners to understand is related to staffing levels, which may include staff retention rates, plans to backfill existing staff, headcount needed to fulfill the new integration's growth plans, or downsizing redundant staff members.

One of our HR M&A Roundtable members tells the story of the acquisition of a small European company by an American multinational. The target company had a high-turnover staffing model that relied on hiring entry-level workers who would remain employed for one to two years. The target's staffing model involved calling a local technical college and asking their best students to fill a role in the organization. Using this model, the target company would usually wait less than a week to backfill any vacancy.

The acquiring company, on the other hand, had a much more robust staffing policy. The average time to fill a requisition in that region was over 75 days. The recruiting process required the manager to leave a job posting open for at least ten days, applicants had to be screened by an internal recruiter, and the hiring manager had to review a minimum number of resumes before interviewing at least three candidates for each opening. The successful candidate would then be subject to a strenuous background check followed by a week of onboarding training before they could start their job.

The onerous staffing model collided with the acquisition's high turnover rate and caused the acquired company to start missing critical customer deadlines. When business leaders began to complain about the problem, the HR practitioner politely showed the leader where the risk appeared in the formal due diligence report, alongside the cost impact of hiring more seasoned professionals who were likely to have more skill and tenure. As the operational risks materialized, the business ended up spending more money solving these problems, which had a direct impact on the business leader's P&L and the deal ROI.

Workforce Quality

HR practitioners should partner with business leaders to understand the quality of the acquired workforce. One of the first steps is looking at the overall staffing trend in the business. Some organizations "clean house" or implement a hiring freeze to prepare for an acquisition. This tactic results in a marked decline in total payroll costs but could result in a situation where individual workloads are too high, and there is an increased risk of attrition or burnout. Absenteeism and other attendance issues are additional types of operational risk.

The acquired workforce may be under-skilled for the current or future operating model. Understanding the performance management model may give some insight into skill levels, but it can be difficult for an HR practitioner to use only PM documents to determine skill gaps. Additional resources include the target company's current job openings, including a review of the recruitment advertisement, which can provide clues about which skills the company feels are necessary to run the business. A thorough review of existing job descriptions might also provide insight into the types of skills the company has historically hired and whether they are appropriate for the post-integration organization. Finally, understanding the target company's training and development programs can provide insight into other areas where the target company believes a skills gap may exist.

One HR M&A Roundtable member knew a workforce problem might exist because the target company had replaced most of its sales organization in the nine months prior to the deal being pursued. The most senior incumbent had less than 18 months of service, and their website advertised several openings for sales team members. The revenue numbers looked good because the target company's services were subject to automatic renewals. However, there was no way the new sales team was going to be able to meet revenue projections. The HR practitioner discussed the situation with the business sponsor and several mitigation options were included in their due diligence report.

Operating Synergies

Most acquisition financial models include both cost and revenue synergies, which we discussed in Chapter 1. For HR practitioners, these synergies are usually realized in business operations. Revenue synergies might involve training employees to cross-sell one another's products or creating a new organizational structure to support marketing re-branded products. Cost synergies may include shutting down locations and laying off employees. HR practitioners should review each synergy in the deal financial model to determine the associated risks.

Chapter 10: Compliance Risk

Compliance risks are those risks that may lead to government-imposed fines or penalties and would likely harm the organization's reputation if the company fails to follow the law or socially accepted employment practices. Compliance risks are usually discovered during the formal due diligence phase, though some may emerge during the target screening phase if compliance issues are made public by employees, regulators, or journalists.

Litigation and Claims

The first step in conducting due diligence for compliance risks includes reviewing any types of claims or litigation for a certain period, often three or five years. Common complaints include those around general employment practices, wrongful termination, wage and hour practices, employee leaves, retaliation, whistleblowing, and numerous other factors. Many buyers are also becoming increasingly sensitive to harassment and discrimination issues in the wake of the #MeToo movement.

The claims review should include both open and closed claims, including any settlement agreements, judgments, or consent decrees. This review should not be limited to complaints filed in the courts or actions taken by regulators. The HR practitioner should also include allegations made using the target company's internal reporting practices, including those that are handled using alternative dispute resolution (ADR), grievance processes, or a third-party arbitrator. It's strongly recommended that an employment attorney review all of these documents regardless of perceived materiality. Unless the HR practitioner is a trained employment attorney, they may not be able to spot issues that could quickly escalate into significant lawsuits.

While closed claims do not present future liabilities in and of themselves, they can provide a great deal of insight into the target company's compliance culture. A review of closed claims against the target company's current employment practices can help determine if past problematic behavior has resolved or if there is a risk that employees or regulators may take further action against the target. Furthermore, this review can help identify any areas of non-compliance that HR will need to handle once the transaction closes.

Employment Terms and Conditions

The next set of documents to have an attorney review consists of employment agreements, consulting agreements, and offer letter templates. It is not uncommon for executive employment agreements to include a change in control provision that governs the employment relationship if there is a sale of the business. For example, an executive or key employee may enjoy accelerated vesting of stock options or receive a transaction bonus. Some executives also have deferred compensation arrangements or special indemnification clauses in their agreements. These arrangements may have tax implications covered under IRS Code section 280G, which provide direction on the tax treatment of "golden parachute" payments. Additionally, these agreements often contain "good reason" clauses, which allow the employee to receive enhanced severances or other special treatment if they resign for a "good reason." Such provisions are often the subject of negotiation since they can affect the acquirer's ability to retain key talent.

For some employees, the offer letter may make specific promises that will be difficult for the acquirer to unwind, such as guaranteed bonus payments or a certain length of employment that could result in increased severance costs if the employee is terminated after the acquisition. Some employment agreements have restrictive covenants such as non-competition, non-solicitation, and non-disclosure agreements. In some jurisdictions, these restrictions are unenforceable or will not transfer to the buyer, meaning the HR practitioner will need to decide if they want to introduce or reintroduce restrictive covenants with acquired employees. Intellectual property ownership is often covered in offer letters or supplemental agreements and should also be examined. A competent employment attorney can help review these issues and determine appropriate mitigations.

An employment attorney should also review all written policies, procedures, and handbooks that affect employees. These documents detail the terms and conditions under which the employer-employee relationship operates, including at-will employment arrangements. They will also address crucial matters related to business ethics, compliance with anti-corruption laws, and reporting and handling of whistleblower complaints. Finally, the buyer needs to understand the progressive discipline and dispute resolution processes, which include mandatory arbitration clauses with increasing frequency.

Have an attorney review all of the target's contingent labor arrangements. Contractors, consultants, gig workers, and other contingent laborers may be de-facto employees who have not been correctly classified and may be subject to employment protections and payment of back wages, back taxes, or penalties. Furthermore, counsel should also assess joint employment arrangements, including professional employer organizations (PEOs), employee leasing companies, staffing agencies, and contract labor arrangements. These arrangements may also result in additional complications and liabilities.

Employee Collective Agreements

Target companies with organized workforces present additional unique issues. A review of collective bargaining agreements, side letters, and memoranda of understanding are essential to a complete due diligence process. These may include collective bargaining obligations that will be assumed by the acquirer or a requirement to negotiate directly with the target company's existing unions. The acquirer will also want to be aware of any lockouts or union actions like strikes or work stoppages, as well as any pending or potential claims of unfair labor practices. Firms that are undergoing collective organizing will also require special treatment during due diligence.

Outside of the United States, employees may be represented not only by trade unions but also by works councils or other employee representative bodies. In any of these cases, the HR practitioner should consult with an appropriate expert.

Other Compliance Matters

A member of the HR organization should review compliance reports, including those related to affirmative action, equal employment opportunity, employment of veterans, and worker safety. A review of all safety training for OSHA compliance, workers' compensation claims, and other health and safety insurance claims, along with unemployment claims history is warranted.

Many HR practitioners find it beneficial to have an attorney review all of the benefits plans provided by the seller. These documents should include paid time off practices in addition to the traditional evaluation of medical and retirement plan documents. Several jurisdictions are introducing mandatory sick time accruals, and many states require the employer to provide leaves for multiple scenarios, including family and medical situations, pregnancy and parental bonding, military service, jury duty, and other circumstances.

Somebody who understands employee classification under the FLSA should evaluate the job descriptions to ascertain if there is a significant risk of misclassification. One HR M&A Roundtable member shared about an acquisition where misclassification of employees resulted in over $2 million in back wage payments. Additionally, wage theft claims are becoming increasingly common, and acquirers will need to be aware of these issues.

With the recent rollout of the European Union's General Data Protection Regulation (GDPR), multinational acquirers are paying more attention to issues of employee data privacy. While the GDPR is currently getting press attention, employee data practices have been a concern for many years. Understanding how the target company manages, handles, stores, disposes of, and protects employee and applicant data should be evaluated during the due diligence process, as violations can be costly and cause extensive reputational harm.

Another area of concern is immigration. If any employees are foreign workers, a change in ownership may affect their visa status or residency applications. The employee census data that was gathered at the beginning of the process should note any employees with work restrictions. It is also vital to verify that the target company complies with laws surrounding employee work authorization, such as the

Immigration Reform and Control Act (IRCA), which requires every employee working in the United States to have an I-9 on file.

One final compliance risk area is associated with employee terminations that may be required to achieve deal synergies. It will be indispensable to understand what types of documents the target company has available to make these types of decisions. Ideally, the target company will have a robust performance management policy that includes regular reviews, as well as performance improvement plans and records related to employee discipline. It will also be critical to understanding the applicable notice and severance requirements when shaping the final cost model and integration plan.

Global Considerations

While many of the basic concepts in this book apply regardless of region, HR must be prepared to account for special compliance considerations in a cross-border deal. For transactions that occur outside of the United States, a prompt understanding of the integration plan is critical because employees in many jurisdictions, especially those in Europe and parts of Asia, enjoy legal protections that employees in the United States do not.

Employment is a fundamental human right in many countries, and the employer-employee relationship is governed by a contract rather than an at-will arrangement. Violating employment law can carry substantial fines and even personal liability, including jail time, in some countries. The financial and personal consequences make it critical to secure counsel who can guide the organization through compliance.

In much of the world, the employment contract and employee handbook strictly govern all employment terms and conditions, including total rewards, which may impact pay mix, benefits, and equity that affect the overall cost model. The total rewards harmonization process takes time and is strictly regulated in many jurisdictions, which may affect the integration timeline. The same applies to how personnel will transfer between employing entities as well as follow on issues related to immigration and work location. There may also be limitations on how redundancies or collective dismissals occur outside the United

States, with requirements that are similar to, but more stringent than, the WARN Act in the US.

Additional things to consider when working outside the United States are the legal rights of works councils, trade unions, and other employee representative bodies which may affect the integration plan. Finally, employment-related intellectual property and restrictive covenants such as non-competes will be treated very differently outside the United States.

Many less sophisticated US-based M&A professionals fail to appreciate the complexities that may arise due to differences in employment laws, and frustrated HR practitioners often try to explain these differences but fail to make their case until problems occur. The best advice for these situations is to understand what the integration plan should look like and rely on employment counsel or HR allies for help. Where possible, explaining the fines and possible jail time associated with a violation can be compelling.

Compliance risks are easy to overlook, but ignoring them can be expensive to remedy, and bad press from failure to follow the law can damage a company's reputation. Ensuring that the right documentation and experts are available to assist the HR team through this process is essential to the deal's success.

Chapter 11: Leadership Risk

Most firms dig deeply into financial factors, operational efficiency, and compliance issues during their due diligence process. Many business sponsors and corporate development professionals only assess these easy-to-quantify elements. They frequently view leadership and culture as soft factors that may be important but are much more difficult and time-consuming to objectively diligence. Many acquirers are at a loss when it comes to rigorous evaluation of leadership and culture, reducing this essential exercise to a brief set of interview questions asked by untrained individuals.

Fortunately, according to observations made by Deloitte[1], acquirers are beginning to see the importance of strong leadership, even though it appears very few organizations have sophisticated ways of evaluating the people who will be responsible for leading the newly acquired company through their upcoming transition and ongoing business operations. Target company leadership should be assessed at every phase in the due diligence process.

One exception to this generality appears to be private equity (PE) firms. David Rubenstein, CEO of the Carlyle Group, has evaluated hundreds of acquired CEOs. In an interview with the Freakonomics podcast, he opined that the quality of the CEO was significantly more important than the purchase price or the quality of the acquired company. Rubenstein will pass on buying a great company with a mediocre CEO in favor of a so-so company with an exemplary CEO[2].

Years of conversations with HR practitioners involved in M&A have led me to one regrettable conclusion: despite the importance of leadership to M&A success, most companies do a terrible job of assessing acquired leaders. Using the ideas in this chapter will help HR practitioners better diligence acquired company leaders.

Deciding Which Leaders to Assess

During the due diligence process, HR practitioners should analyze multiple data sources to learn about the target company. During target screening, pay special attention to the key employees, including their LinkedIn profiles, website biographies, resumes, and Glassdoor feedback. A simple Google search can show if the executive is active in the community or has received any press coverage that might help the HR practitioner understand their leadership competency and how they'll fit within the acquiring organization.

Where possible, use the formal due diligence phase to review the leadership team's performance management information including performance management ratings and 360-degree assessments. If this information is not available, analyze their compensation history to see if pay increases, bonuses, and equity grants can provide any clues about their perceived effectiveness.

In addition to leaders identified on the website and the CIM, the HR practitioner needs to determine if the firm has key person insurance so that everybody the target considers crucial enough to insure is evaluated. Next, they should gather information on succession plans and any leadership development programs the target company has in place to decide if additional employees should be assessed, with particular attention paid to high potential programs. Acquirers frequently pay attention to only executive-level leaders, ignoring next-tier talent that may be more critical to the deal (like the developer mentioned in the introduction). Finally, the post-diligence huddle (Chapter 7) can be used to round out the list of leaders to evaluate.

Research published in Harvard Business Review indicates there are two other populations to consider when evaluating leadership risk[3]. The first population consists of acquired company middle management. The second population includes leaders already inside the acquiring company. Unfortunately, HR practitioners will have a difficult time assessing acquired middle managers during the formal due diligence phase. Middle managers are often unaware of the transaction, so information about them can only be gathered from the target company's deal team or public sources. Even when data is available, the sheer number of middle managers relative to their likely individual impact on deal valuation makes it difficult to justify the time researching them, making robust diligence of this population impractical, if not impossible.

This book focuses on the leadership capabilities of the target company, but acquisition success requires ensuring the acquiring business leaders are ready to manage through integration and value capture. The acquiring company leader must be able to do their day job while simultaneously managing elements of the integration and leading the combined team through significant change.

More sophisticated organizations invest in formal leadership assessments to ensure acquiring organization leaders can do the work associated with the evaluation and integration of an acquired company. At the very least, HR practitioners should facilitate a robust conversation about the readiness of the leader to integrate a new organization, incorporating input from performance management, 360-degree assessments, succession lists, and leadership development plans.

The importance of a deal-ready acquiring team cannot be understated. Some of my most frustrating integrations occurred when the acquiring management team was absent or incompetent, leaving me to wonder why the firm had spent money on a purchase they weren't ready to integrate. Without fail, these deals had lower employee engagement and higher attrition, leading to lower performance, less satisfied customers, and failure to meet the deal's financial objectives.

Leadership Due Diligence Discussion

Using the techniques discussed in Chapter 4, HR practitioners can start researching target company leaders and build a dossier on each person. This research won't provide a comprehensive picture, therefore a separate formal due diligence interview involving the target company's most senior leader and the acquirers' HR practitioner, business sponsors, and corporate development team is recommended. Let the target company leader know which employees will be discussed so they can decide who else to invite. If the acquirer plans to keep the entire leadership team, they should be clear about that upfront, so the target leader understands the meeting is not designed to determine who stays and who goes. If there will be cuts, honesty remains the best policy.

Developing a standard set of questions to ask about each individual will help make the most of limited time. Some sample questions appear below. These questions will need to be modified based on the needs of the acquiring organization.

- Tell me about this person.
- What are their primary duties and responsibilities?
- What are their most important goals? Are they meeting them?
- What do they do well? Where can they use improvement?
- Are they on any succession plans, and do they have a development plan?
- How likely are they to stay on during integration? In the long run?
- What will it take to retain them?
- What are their medium- and long-term career goals?
- Tell me about their team and leadership style.
- What else should we know about this person?

While leadership due diligence interviews will uncover some information about the target company's leadership team, sellers will understandably paint their organization in the best possible light. The CEO's answers about the leadership team will probably be filtered to help close the deal and maximize purchase price. A more robust leadership assessment is necessary to help counteract this effect.

Direct Leadership Observations

Throughout the entire due diligence process, business sponsors, corporate development, HR practitioners, and other functional leaders will have the opportunity to interact with members of the target company leadership team. These interactions may be via email, over the telephone, or face-to-face during meetings, dinners, and site visits. In some cases, members of the acquirer's team will have interacted with target company leaders in other settings, like industry conferences, sales meetings, or even as former colleagues (see Chapter 4 where in-house expertise is addressed). Sophisticated acquirers will take advantage of these opportunities to assess the target company's leaders.

Much like the leadership interview during the formal due diligence phase, the HR practitioner should use a standard set of questions to capture their team's observations of the target company's leaders. Below are some sample questions, which should be modified based on the organization's needs and the nuances of the acquisition. The HR practitioner may also want to add items that reflect the organization's leadership competency model.

- What does the leader's decision-making process look like? Include the factors they appear to consider and how they incorporate diverse stakeholder perspectives, including functional or global views.
- On a scale of 1 to 10, how well can the leader explain critical parts of their business, including key competitors and the overall market? Why did you provide that rating?
- How does the leader react to differences of opinion with you? Changing circumstances? Bad news?
- What role have you seen the leader taking on during meetings? Is their role different when the group size or players change?
- Does the leader keep their commitments to you? Examples include being at meetings on time, returning diligence items on time, and honoring other promises.
- What steps have you noticed the leader taking to motivate their peers and subordinates to complete their work and meet deadlines? How does the leader build trust with their team? Are the interactions you observed consistent with sound leadership practices?
- Have you seen the leader need to clarify a message to an audience? How did they react, and how did it turn out?
- What have your impressions been when watching the leader deliver difficult messages, feedback, or coaching?
- Is there anything else you think we need to know about this leader and how effective they will be during the integration period? In the long run?

Formal Leadership Assessment

Based on conversations with HR M&A Roundtable members, very few strategic acquirers use formal leadership assessment in their leadership due diligence process. However, a growing number of financial acquirers, like private equity (PE) firms, are adding formal leadership assessments as early as the target screening phase. The mantra for many investors is "bet on the jockey, not the horse," leading financial acquirers to invest in formal leadership assessment by the time they reach the formal due diligence phase.

Dr. Dave Ulrich, one of the great HR thinkers of our day, estimates that over 50% of private equity firms have a person dedicated to ensuring formal leadership assessment occurs during a deal[4]. A separate study of PE firms showed that formal evaluation by an independent consultant is more than twice as predictive of leadership success than in-house assessment using structured interviews and background checks.[5]

According to HR M&A Roundtable member Dr. Marc Prine, an industrial and organizational psychologist who performs formal assessments for PE firms, the process begins with an analysis of the acquiring company's needs through the transition and into the final operating state of the acquisition. A custom framework will probably be created for each transaction, as integration models can vary significantly from deal to deal. The consultant will then suggest psychometric instruments that assess personality, leadership style, cognitive ability, motivation, aptitude, grit, and other relevant factors. The online psychometric assessments are followed by an in-depth interview that allows the consultant to assess the leader's ability to handle change, manage stress, navigate through the integration, and assimilate into the final state of the combined company.

The leadership consultant then debriefs both the buyer and the new leader, allowing each party to revisit the framework the leaders were measured against. The conversation includes practical suggestions for building a high performing team that can facilitate a smoother integration and make value capture more likely. This approach can reduce role ambiguity, level set performance expectations, and ensure the buyer and seller are on the same page.

While some firms bring leadership assessment in-house, most use outside consulting firms that have knowledge and expertise across industries to perform the evaluation. An outside firm is generally best suited to help determine which tests are relevant and predictive for an organization and can help the HR practitioner avoid the legal challenges associated with pre-employment testing in some jurisdictions.

Types of Leadership Risks

Leadership risks arise when a leader is either unwilling or unable to complete the integration or operate the business in the long-term. Retention risk refers to the likelihood of the leader exiting the company shortly after the transaction closes. Retention planning is covered at length in Chapter 18, along with an extensive list of options to incentivize leaders to remain onboard through integration or ongoing operations. Obviously, a leader who exits is not able to take the acquired company through the forthcoming change.

The remaining element of leadership risk emerges when a leader is not able to manage the business through integration or ongoing operations. Ultimately, the HR practitioner must assess the acquired company leaders' ability to help their team integrate smoothly, execute on the business plan, and assimilate into the acquiring company's culture.

According to recent research by The Conference Board[6], leaders draw on different skills as the deal progresses through its various phases. During the formal due diligence and integration planning phases, the leader needs to demonstrate more hard skills, such as deep understanding of their business, financial acumen, customer focus, strategic thinking, and sound judgment. Soft skills are less critical, but a baseline ability to communicate, inspire trust, and lead teams is necessary. During their early interactions, business sponsors and corporate development teams see these competencies play out. A target company leader who doesn't demonstrate these skills may not be able to close the deal!

As they work toward integrating the business and working toward value capture, the acquired leader will need to evolve their awareness of the external market and customer needs into specific planning and execution to ensure they grow market share and revenues. Internally, their soft skills will be tested as they lead through meaningful organizational change, build new relationships, and lead combined teams. Furthermore, this research shows that soft skills become significantly more important than hard skills during integration. The business sponsor and corporate development team have fewer opportunities to see the soft skills, which is why the interviews, observations, and formal assessments are critical to predicting the leader's ability to deliver on deal value.

One HR M&A Roundtable member told the story of a leader who had all the right answers when the company was being sold, but wasn't able to effectively lead through integration. The target company CEO was an excellent salesman who had been part of several M&As throughout his career. He understood the value of his company, had all of the documents lined up, and turned on the charm to get the best price possible for his company.

Unfortunately, when the time came for him to communicate with his employees, he fell flat. The CEO had a reputation for selling too much, and the employees didn't trust him to tell them the truth. The corporate development team saw his more acerbic personality traits come through during a few negotiation calls, but dismissed it as irrelevant. This left the business sponsor and HR practitioner scrambling to do damage control and find others who could shepherd the team through integration and help stem the loss of talent that was starting to occur.

If the HR practitioner has any doubts about the acquired leader's capabilities in these areas, they should capture the risk in their formal due diligence report, along with a proposed mitigation plan, such as providing an executive coach, assigning a strong chief of staff, or even replacing the acquired leader with somebody from the acquiring company.

Chapter 12: Culture Risk

Researchers and business leaders have been discussing the importance of culture in M&A since at least the 1960s[1], making it ironic that M&A leaders are still debating its importance decades later, with many executives asserting that the fundamental economic model and strong operational strategy matter more[2]. This either/or divide between culture and strategy ignores the reality that *both* culture *and* strategy are critical to business success, even if M&A isn't part of the picture.

If we simplify the risks outlined in Part Three of this book, we can say financial opportunities are *why* we do a deal, operations tell us *what* we are doing, leadership tells us *who* will be accountable, and culture tells us *how* to make it happen.

Unless a business is left entirely standalone, merely becoming a part of the acquirer's portfolio with no input whatsoever from the buyer, then something is going to change. Assessing culture risk allows the acquirer to determine how easy the change is likely to be and which change levers to pull.

Remember, many organizations don't appreciate the word "culture." Substitute phrases like "operational readiness" or "integration challenges" may make it easier to discuss this topic. A culturally similar target company is probably more ready to embrace the proposed operating model. A culturally different target company will likely experience more integration challenges.

Like leadership, culture can be assessed at every phase of due diligence. During target screening, the acquiring team will see how the organization operates via their website, in media mentions, and through its leaders. During formal due diligence, they will see the culture through the handbook, policies and procedures, and the target organizations interactions with the team. With interaction through integration planning and integration, the team will continue to learn about the company's culture and how it will support or hinder value capture.

Understanding Cultural Differences

The first step in understanding culture risk is evaluating how each organization does business. If the transaction is designed to be transformational or involves multiple parties, the HR practitioner will also need to understand the desired cultural end state.

HR practitioners who are well versed in culture and organizational development may consider the cultural elements uncovered in M&A to be more about climate than culture. While this distinction is useful for specialized practitioners, the two constructs are often confounded in practice. To ensure focus remains on the important work of assessing organizational differences and using that information to lead through change, this book uses culture as a blanket term that incorporates culture and climate.

It's impossible to detail each area where organizational cultures will differ, but here are a few of the more significant organizational culture dimensions that come up in M&A[3].

- How are power and authority distributed in the organization?
- Who has the right to make what kinds of decisions?
- How are decisions made?
- What accountability mechanisms exist?
- How does day-to-day work get done?
- What are the team dynamics like?
- How well is the organization connected internally?
- Does the company focus more on results or processes?
- How do leaders communicate?
- What does the organization want employees to focus on?
- What is the physical environment like?
- How does the organization celebrate major events?

In addition to organizational differences, the HR practitioner will need to understand if there are significant national or regional cultures that operate in the background. Even if organizations are nearly identical in each of the areas mentioned above, there may still be challenges if one party is in New York and the other is in Seattle. A Wall Street executive who insists on wearing an expensive suit while talking with a group of Seattle software developers is likely to get eye-rolls on the way out. Similarly, a San Francisco operations leader with purple hair and orange sneakers will have a hard time being taken seriously when first meeting her new team in Atlanta.

These geographic differences will be even more exacerbated if one group is in Poland and the other in Nashville. A recent study showed the cultural differences between Japanese acquirers and their western target companies resulted in financial performance that was 12% lower than western targets acquired by western companies[4]. Japanese firms prefer a centralized leadership approach where hard plans are made and seldom revised, whereas American and European companies tend to use less stringent roadmaps that require line managers to have more autonomy.

As firms mature their M&A processes, they begin to look at cultural differences to improve their chances of successfully recognizing the deal thesis. The HR M&A Roundtable website (www.MandARoundtable.com) has a cultural assessment tool that can guide HR practitioners through this process.

Change Agility

Once the HR practitioner understands the organizational differences, they will have better awareness of the magnitude of the proposed change. They will have a sense of the target's ability to change along with an understanding of important cultural markers.

Some organizations are more ready for change than others, and some types of change are more comfortable to navigate than others. During the due diligence process, the HR practitioner will want to evaluate how ready the target company is to transition from its current state to the proposed end state. This analysis requires them to understand the desired end state, which means they should have at least some sense of the final operating model for the combined business.

Public information is an excellent place to start. Be sure to include what the company says about itself in press releases and on its website. Analyze past change events and evaluate how the company has dealt with shifts. Follow this up by reviewing Glassdoor feedback and seeing if there is any news coverage about the organization. Next, look at documents the company provides, including engagement and exit survey data alongside turnover and retention information. Compliance reports and litigation can also provide clues about the organization's climate and readiness to change. As the process continues, HR may find that employees are ready to change some things, but not others.

Change Levers

Using information gained during diligence, the HR practitioner can begin to consider the steps necessary to move how the acquired company does business now to the desired end state, leveraging leaders, business practices, communications, and other resources. Further exploration of the change plan is outside the scope of this book, but HR practitioners can learn more by joining the HR M&A Roundtable.

If the HR practitioner doesn't have this capability, they should consider working with a change management expert. A surprising number of M&A deals fail due to cultural issues. If there are doubts about changing how the company will get its work done, it should be captured as a culture risk.

Chapter 13: HR Functional Risk

The first five risk areas address how people, leadership, and culture affect the company. The last risk area is how HR manages HR in the acquired company and how HR services will be delivered post-integration. HR practitioners will learn about the target company's HR function during every stage, but will gain the most information on their HR function during formal due diligence.

The primary responsibility of the HR function is managing the employee lifecycle. This includes attracting, recruiting, selecting, onboarding, evaluating, remunerating, rewarding, developing, engaging, retaining, and exiting employees. The effects of the front-end of the employee lifecycle (attracting, recruiting, selecting, and onboarding employees) alongside evaluating and developing employees are discussed with operational risk in Chapter 9. Remunerating and rewarding employees are discussed in Chapter 8 on financial risk. Employee engagement and retention are covered alongside leadership risk in Chapter 11 and cultural risk in Chapter 12. Retirement and severance implications of employee exits are discussed in Chapter 8 (financial risk), and legal implications are covered in Chapter 10 (compliance risk).

Merely understanding the risks associated with managing the employee lifecycle does not guarantee that HR function is up to the job, making it critical to diligence the HR function and its ability to deliver HR services into the current and future organization.

The first step is understanding how HR services are delivered at the target company. Some organizations will have a fully functioning HR team, where others may relegate HR responsibility to the CFO, office manager, or third parties. Once the acquiring HR team understands the HR operating model, they can assess how well-equipped the HR organization is to navigate the integration process and support the final state of the combined business.

Most organizations engage a significant number of HR vendors. These include HR information systems, recruitment and applicant tracking systems, job boards, recruiting and staffing firms, payroll providers, benefits and insurance companies, training providers, employment attorneys, outside consultants, survey providers, and a variety of other products and services. The HR practitioner will need to determine which vendors will need to stay on through integration and into the final business model.

If the target company's HR function lacks the talent, tools, or capacity to work through integration and support the ultimate business combination, the acquiring HR practitioner should capture the risk in their formal due diligence report and develop appropriate mitigation proposals.

Chapter 14: Assessing HR Risks

At this point in the transaction, the HR practitioner will have gathered scads of information and organized it into one of six risk areas. The next step will require a determination of how significant the risks are, which will, in turn, allow development of a proposed mitigation strategy, should mitigation be required.

A risk must be relevant, likely, and material to merit attention. Most business sponsors only consider a risk relevant if it affects the deal financial model, integration timing, company reputation, or talent retention. Likelihood refers to the probability of a risk coming to fruition.

Materiality refers to the size of the risk in relation to the broader business context, including the purchase price. For example, an HR practitioner could discover that the front desk person may be misclassified and is therefore entitled to $2,500 in back wages. In the context of a $50 million acquisition, that cost is probably immaterial. On the other hand, a $1.5 million underfunded pension liability would be material for most M&A transactions.

Risk Assessment Matrix

The risk assessment matrix is a widely used project management tool that allows the user to visually plot the probability of a risk occurring along with the likely impact that will result if the risk comes to fruition. This tool is also frequently called a probability-impact matrix or heat map, among other names. A traditional risk assessment matrix is a five-by-five table showing the impact on one axis and the probability on the other.

The matrix shared in this section is most useful for plotting financial, integration timing, and reputational risks. Talent retention risks use a similar model, which is detailed in Chapter 18. It may be that the acquiring company or the industry it's in is sensitive to risks that aren't outlined in this section. If that is the case, the matrix should be modified accordingly. Depending on the size and complexity of the deal, it may make sense to create a separate chart for each risk. Like many tools, the heat map can be highly subjective, and professional judgment will have to be applied when using it.

Sample Risk Assessment Matrix

Probability ↕	Impact ← →	Negligible	Minor	Moderate	Major	Significant
	Almost Certain	⚠	⚠	⊗	⊗	⊗
	Likely	⚠	⚠	⚠	⊗	⊗
	Possible	✓	⚠	⚠	⚠	⊗
	Unlikely	✓	✓	⚠	⚠	⚠
	Improbable	✓	✓	✓	⚠	⚠

Impact

Risk impact refers to the severity of the consequences that will arise if the risk occurs. The more extreme the risk, the higher the point value. The table below outlines one way of plotting financial, integration timing, and reputational risks on the heat map. The organization's financial materiality thresholds and risk tolerance may require customization of this approach.

Impact Ratings

Rating	Financial Impact	Timing Impact	Reputational Impact
5 (Significant)	More than 1% of deal value	Integration may not occur at all.	Irreparable damage to company brand. Customers and employees flee.
4 (Major)	0.5% to 1% of deal value	Integration schedule will slip significantly.	Significant damage control required. Customers and employees raise concerns in public.
3 (Moderate)	0.25% to 0.5% of deal value	The integration may be slightly delayed.	Some effort and expense required to restore customer and employee trust.
2 (Minor)	0.1% to 0.25% of deal value	Delays will be easy to recover.	Minimal damage to company brand.
1 (Negligible)	Less than 0.1% of deal value	The schedule will remain on track.	No significant impact on customer and employee perception.

Probability

The next step is estimating the likelihood of a risk occurring. Estimating risk requires HR practitioners to imagine future scenarios that may not feel familiar. If the probability score is not apparent, the due diligence team should talk it over. The chart below provides a few ways to consider probability. HR practitioners should choose the scale that works best for the deal or develop a rubric that works in their organization.

Probability Ratings

Rating	Percentage	Frequency	Complexity
5 (Almost Certain)	Greater than 90%	Occurs at least once a quarter.	Almost guaranteed to happen.
4 (Likely)	65% to 90%	Occurs a few times per year.	Will probably happen if a common factor arises.
3 (Possible)	35% to 65%	Occurs every six months to one year.	May or may not happen.
2 (Unlikely)	10% to 35%	Occurs once every one to two years.	Requires an unusual combination of factors to happen.
1 (Improbable)	Less than 10%	Occurs less than once every two years.	Will happen only under rare conditions.

Since due diligence happens in phases, the risk assessment matrix will be populated in phases. The sample risk assessment matrix in this chapter will help the HR practitioner to understand which risks are likely to emerge in different deal phases and how they are placed on the matrix. How to develop mitigation proposals for these risks will be covered in Part 5 of the book.

Sample Risk Assessment Matrix

	Negligible	Minor	Moderate	Major	Significant
Almost Certain	⚠ 3.1	⚠	⊗ 2.1	⊗	⊗ 1.1
Likely	⚠	⚠	⚠ 2.2	⊗	⊗
Possible	⊘	⚠	⚠ 2.3	⚠	⊗
Unlikely	⊘	⊘	⚠	⚠ 1.2	⚠
Improbable	⊘	⊘ 3.2	⊘	⚠	⚠

Impact →
Probability ↑

Target Screening

The objective of target screening is to determine whether a preliminary offer will be made via the LOI. HR's job at this point is to identify deal killers and inputs to the financial model. Target screening includes considering executive retention which is covered in Chapter 18.

Based on HR's review of public information and the CIM, the following risks are identified.

- Risk 1.1: The target company CIM shows a retiree medical plan that is not adequately funded. It will cost $12M to fund the plan. The risk is almost certain and the impact is significant due to its total cost to remedy.
- Risk 1.2: Analysis of Glassdoor and social media mentions show target company employees are motivated by their social values, which are expressed differently than the acquiring company's social values. It is possible, but unlikely, that the employees may choose to protest by quitting or organizing, which the company would consider a major impact. This challenge cannot be resolved using targeted retention incentives, so it is included in this risk matrix.

Formal Due Diligence

The formal due diligence phase gives the acquiring company additional access to the target's leaders, sites, and documents. The HR practitioner will use this information to identify potential deal killers, inputs to the financial model, or changes to the definitive agreement. This is also when they will start working on retention of key employees (covered in Chapter 18).

While working on formal due diligence, a few risks that are relevant to the deal are discovered.

- Risk 2.1: When discussing target company headcount with the finance team, it's learned that the synergy plan requires two factories to combine, resulting in job losses and triggering WARN notices. Additionally, one of the firm's major customers is in this town. The risk is almost certain to occur and it will take time and money to rebuild customer and employee trust.
- Risk 2.2: During the due diligence interview, it's mentioned that one of the European locations is represented by a works council. A labor attorney is consulted and says that the works council must be consulted before the deal can go forward. The works council is likely to approve the plan, but will probably impose

some conditions, making this risk likely to emerge. The labor expert assumes the deal timeline will slide one to two months, which is a moderate impact.

- Risk 2.3: During the post-diligence huddle, there's news that attrition in the target's R&D department is twice as high as attrition in the acquirer's R&D department. If attrition continues at the current pace, and time to fill remains the same, critical R&D roles will be vacant for long periods of time, which may affect product release milestones. HR estimates the risk is 40% likely to emerge, meaning the risk is possible. If the risk emerges, the impact will be moderate due to loss of customer trust and timeline challenges.

Integration Planning

After the deal is signed and announced, the HR practitioner will have broader access to the target company's team members. While they will still look for potential deal killers and items with a financial impact, their primary focus will be understanding how to integrate the target company in accordance with the integration plan. While this section focuses on risks, don't forget the goal of the integration plan is to help the company meet its financial objectives for the acquisition.

As the HR practitioner works with other members of the deal team, they identify the following risks:

- Risk 3.1: When reviewing job descriptions, HR discovers the office manager in one location is probably misclassified under the FLSA. Back wages will be approximately $10,000. This risk is almost certain to occur, but the cost is negligible in the overall context of the deal.
- Risk 3.2: During a conversation with the target's HR leader, they learn the target cannot find intellectual property agreements for several back-office employees. The risk of an issue emerging is improbable since the employees did not work directly on any products and did not have access to trade secrets. The impact of an issue arising would be minor for the same reason.

Retention risks are not included in this list. A slightly different risk matrix for retention planning is shared in Chapter 18.

As you reviewed this list, you may have already started thinking about ways to mitigate these risks. In addition to the solutions you're probably considering, the M&A process provides several unique options for risk mitigation that do not occur in day-to-day HR work. Part 4 of the book covers the most common risk mitigation options available to HR practitioners.

Part 4: Mitigating HR Risks

A t the beginning of this book, we stated that:

Due Diligence is the art and science of identifying, assessing, and mitigating risks associated with an M&A transaction.

The final step in managing the due diligence process is developing appropriate mitigations for the risks that emerge. Risks that are highly likely and highly impactful will require a more severe mitigation approach than risks that have a lower level of either likelihood or impact.

The following chapters offer risk mitigation approaches HR practitioners should consider when finalizing the due diligence process. The most extreme risk mitigation option is to kill the deal. After that, HR practitioners can explore altering the contract terms, and finally we'll discuss changing the integration plan. This list provides information on the most common methods for reducing or eliminating the risks that have been identified, but it is not exhaustive. HR practitioners will need to apply their best professional judgment and knowledge of their organizations and acquisitions to be successful.

Retention risks present additional unique opportunities and retention plans can be made at several points during the deal process. We'll explore retention planning in the last chapter of this part.

Chapter 15: Kill the Deal

The first and most apparent mitigation option is to terminate the transaction. Death of a deal is a common occurrence during the due diligence process. According to Forbes, approximately half of all proposed M&A transactions are terminated during the due diligence process[1]. Ending the M&A process is usually related to material financial matters and most frequently happens during target identification and formal due diligence. On rare occasions, a deal can be killed after the parties sign the definitive agreement, but that requires a finding so significant the buyer can invoke the material adverse change clause of the contract, which is very difficult to do.

It is highly unusual for a deal to die based on human resource issues alone; however, there are rare circumstances when HR risks become deal killers. Not surprisingly, this typically involves events that carry significant financial or reputational risks, such as ongoing union disputes or current organizing activity, serious employment litigation, issues with ownership of intellectual property, or pension liability funding challenges.

HR-related operational risks may also become deal killers. A deal may die if the workforce isn't ready to execute on the proposed integration plan, or there is little faith that the acquired leaders will be able to turn around a distressed operating unit or adapt to the new organizational culture.

One of our HR M&A Roundtable members shared a situation where a significant pension liability would need to be assumed by the acquirer. In this case, the potential buyer was unwilling to take on a defined benefit pension plan, and the seller wasn't willing to reduce the purchase price enough to offset the pension liability and make the deal attractive. The transaction didn't go through.

A second situation involved leadership and culture mismatch. The buyer and seller had vastly different leadership styles. The buyer didn't trust the seller to be the change champion they needed to integrate the company successfully and smoothly. Furthermore, there were significant concerns that key talent would follow the acquired CEO to his next opportunity, which would result in a considerable decrease in deal value.

HR practitioners shouldn't expect to use the nuclear option very often. Instead, HR practitioners should focus on less severe possibilities for mitigating the risks that emerge during the due diligence process.

Chapter 16: Change the Deal Terms and Conditions

Shortly after completion of the formal due diligence phase, corporate development teams and deal attorneys will negotiate the final contract between the parties involved in the sale. This document is called by many names, including the purchase and sale agreement, asset purchase agreement, or stock purchase agreement; for simplicity, we'll refer to it as the definitive agreement.

The definitive agreement will include financial aspects of the transaction, representations and warranties, and a series of covenants or promises which the parties agree to make with one another. It will also include remedies for breaches, including indemnifications and exit clauses.

These documents tend to be relatively lengthy and are subject to intense negotiation between the parties. Most sophisticated acquirers engage their HR organizations early in the contract review process, allowing the HR team to review the agreement and provide input into employee matters. When terminating the transaction isn't an appropriate mitigation strategy, the HR practitioner may need to influence specific provisions of the definitive agreement as a result of their due diligence findings.

This chapter will review the significant parts of the definitive agreement and share some insights into how each section might be used to mitigate some of the risks found in due diligence. HR practitioners have an interest in each of these sections, making it critical to review the document in light of the information collected.

Financial Elements and Deal Structure

The first, and some would argue most critical, part of the definitive agreement is the purchase price and transaction type. This section lays out which legal entities are part of the transaction and how the transaction will be consummated amongst those entities. Sometimes this is a simple sale of shares or assets between one company and another. Other times the deal structure requires several attorneys and tax advisors to decipher. HR has a vested interest in understanding this because the transaction type may dictate how employees transfer from seller to buyer, especially in countries that have employment protection legislation.

Other financial matters that may appear in the definitive agreement dictate how existing equity gets treated. In addition to how each side of the transaction will manage shares and options, this may include details on financial retention schemes such as holdbacks and earnouts, which are discussed in Chapter 18.

Adjust the Purchase Price

On occasion, an HR finding may be so significant that it warrants an adjustment to the purchase price rather than a specific indemnity. HR-related purchase price adjustments don't occur very often, and close coordination with the corporate development team will be required. To make a purchase price adjustment, the value of the assets and liabilities must significantly change relative to the deal thesis. A valuation change may occur if there are underfunded pension liabilities, retiree medical liabilities, severance considerations, or significant unpaid employee entitlements such as sick or vacation time that the buyer must assume.

Even if the change isn't significant enough to warrant a purchase price adjustment, the HR practitioner will still want to share the financial findings with the corporate development team at the end of each phase so they can adjust the economic model for the acquisition. Specific contributions HR makes to the deal financial model were discussed in Chapter 8.

Change the Deal Structure

In some cases, the level of risk associated with an HR item will require modification of not only those sections related to employees, but the overall structure of the transaction. For example, to ensure the seller keeps certain employee liabilities, a firm may choose to buy only select assets of the target company rather than engage in a stock sale. The asset deal can effectively isolate certain employment liabilities from the buyer and may help to mitigate some types of significant risk.

One member of the HR M&A Roundtable was able to convince their corporate deal team to change a share sale to an asset sale to significantly reduce the severance liability that would result from significant layoffs that would be required to achieve the cost synergies in the deal's financial model. Her company usually only conducted stock purchases, and the idea of an asset sale was very different for them. Because she was able to estimate the total cost of the severances and present them in the language of the business, she changed the way her company looked at this transaction.

The change from a share sale to an asset sale or vice-versa may impact the mechanism for employment transfers in some parts of the world, so this example is very nuanced. Furthermore, in some countries, it is not lawful to terminate employees simply because of an M&A event. Engage an employment attorney who understands employment transfer legislation in the relevant jurisdictions before adjusting the deal structure.

Representations, Warranties, and Indemnities

Definitive agreements also include a section called representations and warranties. A "rep" is a statement of fact which the company warrants is accurate. HR practitioners will usually want guarantees that the company complies with all laws and regulations, has correctly classified employees, and is managing payroll taxes appropriately. A growing number of buyers are also requesting representations around sexual harassment in light of the #MeToo movement.

Tightly coupled with the reps and warranties are the disclosure schedules. These disclosures list out, or schedule, important information the seller needs to disclose to the buyer for the transaction to go forward. The buyer may schedule major customers, critical suppliers, and employee information. They often include an inventory of exceptions to the reps and warranties, such as a list of employees who have not executed an intellectual property agreement.

While it can be a painful exercise, somebody on the HR team must compare the disclosure schedules to the information gathered during due diligence. Failing to reconcile this information could result in additional employees being added to the transaction, raising payroll costs, or critical employees could suddenly end up left out, eliminating a valuable source of talent. Other changes might also occur, like the addition of benefits plans or insurance programs that the HR practitioner was unaware of. Any material differences between the diligence provided and the schedules reviewed should cast doubt on much of the information gathered in due diligence, and the transaction should be examined in light of this fact.

Depending on the findings, HR practitioners may want to influence the deal reps and warranties. Generally, the buyer wants a broad representation, and the seller wants a little wiggle room. For example, if HR is concerned that the seller doesn't have performance management documents for every employee, and they are relying on those documents for layoffs, they might request a specific representation that the company is following the performance management policy and has adequate documentation.

There are financial consequences (indemnities) for providing an inaccurate rep or warranty, providing some relief to the buyer if the company experiences material harm as a result of a bad rep. However, these penalties often have a ceiling and may not exceed a certain amount. For some HR risks, it may be advisable to create a specific indemnity with a different financial penalty for a breach. Some buyers may request the seller place all or part of an indemnity in escrow for a specified period. Specific indemnities and escrows are usually reserved for significant matters, such as sexual harassment, pending litigation, or employee misclassification.

Covenants and Closing Conditions

The final section of the definitive agreement to be discussed includes a set of covenants or promises between the parties. These covenants often prohibit the company from spending large amounts of money or making any significant changes. This covenant ensures the buyer is getting the business in roughly the same condition that it was in during due diligence. Some sellers request covenants from the buyer, including obligations to treat employees in a specific manner. Requested covenants may include anything from payment of retention or transaction bonuses to the continuation of a particularly popular benefit. HR should always review the agreement before it is signed to ensure they can keep the promises the company is making and to ensure no additional information is scheduled on the final agreement.

HR practitioners may be able to mitigate some risks by modifying closing conditions for the transaction. Again, this process is very similar to buying a home. If a home inspector finds maintenance issues, the buyer may ask the seller to handle them before the seller agrees to close on the purchase. The same thing can happen when purchasing a company.

Some closing conditions are considered fairly standard for an M&A transaction. For example, there may be regulatory approvals required before a sale can close. The parties will each agree that antitrust filings must be made and approved by the government before the transaction can be consummated.

Additionally, it is not uncommon for the buyer to require that the seller not make any decisions that result in a material adverse change, meaning those decisions have a significantly negative effect on the business. The seller essentially promises it won't do anything to reduce the value of the company unless the buyer agrees. There is often a fine line here, as buyers aren't permitted to dictate the operations of the seller until after the transaction closes. When the buyer and seller engage in certain types of joint conduct before the close of the sale, they may be "gun jumping," which violates antitrust law. The acquiring company's legal team can share more information on gun jumping if the HR practitioner has concerns.

Other closing conditions can be related to cleaning up issues that are discovered during the due diligence process. For example, the buyer may request the seller collect intellectual property and non-disclosure agreements from employees if they are not on file. Until the seller gathers those documents, the deal will not close. Other common closing conditions include having key employees waive change in control clauses in their employment contracts, requiring a certain number of named employees to accept new employment offers, or settling outstanding employment litigation before the deal can close.

For asset deals, the buyer may ask the seller to "ringfence" employee populations, ensuring critical talent cannot be moved to other parts of the organization and must transfer to the buyer as part of the transaction.

Modify Post-Closing Covenants

The seller may insist on certain post-closing covenants in the agreement. These post-closing covenants require the buyer to treat employees in a certain way. If these covenants affect people in the transaction, the HR team should consult with an employment attorney to ensure the language makes sense, and the acquirer is confident they can keep their promises.

It is not uncommon for the buyer and seller to negotiate total rewards covenants in excruciating detail. While it may not seem significant, the difference between benefits that are "no less favorable" and benefits that are "at least equivalent in the aggregate" is meaningful for many transactions.

In some cases, the seller will also request that transferring employees have job protections ensuring they remain on the buyer's payroll for a certain amount of time. This timeframe often aligns with legislation governing successor liability for termination and severance costs. Essentially, the seller is attempting to make the buyer fully responsible for the burden of restructuring the business if necessary. The HR practitioner should work with the corporate development team and employment counsel to ensure the contract language does what they intend for it to do.

Transition Service Agreements

From time to time, the buyer and seller will enter into a transition service agreement (TSA). The TSA is not part of the definitive agreement but is a standalone document that requires the seller to provide specific services to the buyer for a set period of time. Companies usually use TSAs in deals where only part of the seller's business is moving to the buyer, for example, when a company is selling only one of their factories or is shedding a specific line of business.

TSAs are usually straightforward documents. The seller will continue to support the business they are selling, and the buyer will pay them for that support. Employee-facing services frequently covered by a TSA include payroll and benefits, IT services like email and network infrastructure, and office services if the employees will not immediately move to a location controlled by the buyer.

HR practitioners should understand the provisions of the TSA, as they may affect the integration timeline. The HR practitioner should also consider if a TSA is necessary, as they may be able to better address the challenges by engaging a professional employer organization (PEO) or employee leasing company. Finally, an employment attorney should review the TSA, as the arrangement may be illegal in some jurisdictions and create additional liabilities in others.

Chapter 17: Leverage the Integration Plan

The most common way to address the HR risks identified during due diligence is through the integration plan. HR practitioners must develop their plan inside the context of the overall transition plan and the final business operating model. Most elements of the integration plan will be worked in conjunction with the IMO and other functions, making coordination with other leaders imperative.

This chapter addresses some of the primary elements of a sound integration strategy but will not replace a full integration plan or an HR M&A playbook. Serial acquirers should develop a living playbook that guides HR practitioners through the stages of a deal while still providing flexibility to manage the nuances of each transaction. Participation in continuing education and peer-learning forums like the HR M&A Roundtable can help HR practitioners develop skill in this area as learning from others is an excellent way to evolve both personal and organizational capability, which ultimately allows for development of more effective integration plans.

Finally, it's important to remember the goal of the integration plan is to ensure the company is able to make more money because of the merger or acquisition. The plan should consider how HR will support value capture through revenue and cost synergies, not just how it will be used to mitigate risks found during the due diligence process.

Organizational Structure

The first step in supporting the future operating model will be an organizational structure that can deliver on deal value. The easiest way to communicate the structure is an organizational chart that includes names and reporting relationships. Providing job descriptions that clearly define each leaders' roles, responsibilities, and decision rights will further support the organization's design.

When possible, share the subordinate organizational structure with the leader. This information should include future headcount, including the names of people who will be invited to remain in the future organization and people who will be asked to exit. If individual decisions have not yet been made, try to provide a list of future roles and headcounts. Bringing the future organizational structure into being will also require HR practitioners to execute the retention plan. If headcount reductions are proposed, the termination timeline and severance requirements must also be considered in the final integration model.

Employer of Record, Pay, and Benefits

Once the HR practitioner has identified which employees will remain, they will need to determine how to pay those employees and what benefits they will receive. This decision process must include determinations about which legal entity will be the employer of record and how and when employees will transfer between the entities if necessary. This step will also require the HR team to design the future total rewards structure, including any changes to base pay, incentives, equity, benefits, and perks, as well as possible alignment of employees into the buyer's job architecture.

In some cases, the acquirer may not be able to make these decisions unilaterally. Collective bargaining agreements, works council consultations, and employee transfer legislation must all be considered in the integration timeline.

Synergy Realization

As we've discussed, recognizing deal value may require HR interventions other than changing organizational design and reward structures. Supporting positive synergies may include developing and delivering programs that cross-train sales employees or teach factory workers how to operate new equipment. On the flip side, HR may need to model severance costs and work on exiting or redeploying workers. HR practitioners should work with their business sponsors and corporate development teams to see how the HR function can support synergy realization.

Communications and Change Leadership

The HR organization is often responsible for coordinating employee communications and helping managers lead through change. M&A is one of the most challenging life events most employees will ever endure. HR practitioners should work to ensure that the acquiring company treats each employee with dignity and respect.

If the acquiring organization lacks the resources to lead change effectively, engage the services of an outside expert. A poor employee experience will result in lower engagement, which in turn generates higher turnover, reduced productivity, and lower customer satisfaction. Ineffective change leadership will affect the acquired firm's revenues and profits, destroying value instead of creating it.

HR Service Delivery

Finally, HR must decide how critical HR services will be delivered into the future organization. This will require a plan for the HR organizational structure, headcount, and systems.

Rely on HR Fundamentals

As HR practitioners work through the due diligence process, they will encounter strange situations and will need to rely on their HR expertise to manage those challenges. One HR M&A Roundtable member dealt with a seller whose primary concern was a job for his son who had just finished graduate school. Another had a works council form right after the acquisition was announced. None of these situations were day-to-day HR, but handling them required a strong grasp of HR fundamentals.

Unusual things will happen as you work through M&A, just as they will happen in any other HR role. Your best plans will need to change. Be flexible and trust your instincts. Putting common sense solutions in place will make all the difference in your integration planning.

Chapter 18: Provide Retention Incentives

Retention plans are a specific way of mitigating operational, leadership, and culture risks in a transaction. Retention incentives are a crucial part of the M&A ecosystem and are usually considered separately from other types of HR risks for a variety of reasons that are both practical and political.

Retention issues emerge at every stage of due diligence. During target screening, HR should determine which top executives should be mentioned in the LOI. The formal due diligence phase provides an opportunity to look at retention options for other critical leaders. As integration planning proceeds, HR can look deeper into the organization. Finally, if additional retention incentives are indicated as integration moves forward, HR can work to ensure they are put into place.

M&A activity creates unique environments in which employees must operate, significantly increasing the risk of flight. The work environment often becomes chaotic and uncertain, and employees grasp for a sense of stability and identity in the swirl. Left unmanaged, the work environment becomes increasingly toxic, creating what HR M&A Roundtable member Mark Walztoni[1] refers to as the *triple bump.* In the triple bump, the "A" players leave within weeks of the deal announcement. The second bump occurs when the firm has a difficult time finding new talent because the organization has earned a bad reputation. The third bump occurs when the remaining employees—usually the "B" and "C" players—are so disengaged they stop creating value.

The leadership retention picture isn't any better. A longitudinal study of 23,000 executives in 1,000 target firms found that leadership attrition in merged firms is more than double that of comparable enterprises. Even more concerning, this effect can last up to a decade post-merger![2]

Outside recruiters are aware of this dynamic and will exploit this weakness in the organization. During one HR M&A Roundtable presentation, M&A leadership consultant Dr. Marc Prine said: "If headhunters are sharks, an acquisition announcement is blood in the water." A solid retention plan can frustrate bloodthirsty recruiters, reducing the likelihood of the triple bump and the downstream financial and operational risks it generates.

Retention plans provide both financial and non-financial incentives for employees to remain with the buyer for a certain amount of time. There are many opinions about the right way to incentivize employees to stay after a transaction is announced, and the buyer will need to develop plans that make sense for their industry, company, and purchase. This section is designed to highlight the process of developing a retention plan that will help you mitigate people-related risks and achieve deal value.

Synthesize the Findings

During target screening and formal due diligence, the HR practitioner probably collected information on the critical roles and competencies required to integrate, lead, and operate the combined business. The key leaders and contributors were identified for each function and a sense of their risk of flight during the relevant timeframe developed. If this couldn't be done during due diligence, the HR practitioner will need to play catch up to make sure these critical individuals stay when the headhunters start calling!

The first step in the creation of a successful retention program is understanding what the business needs to realize the deal thesis. It's a good idea to segment retention tasks by time horizon, first looking at retention needs during the integration period and then at longer-term retention requirements. Successfully performing this analysis will depend a great deal on the integration plan. Consultation with the business sponsor and IMO will be critical to understanding the timeframe for retention arrangements. Segmenting the population by time horizon allows HR practitioners to design incentives that are appropriate to the business risk they are trying to mitigate. It will also provide an opportunity to evaluate populations that are solving similar operational challenges at the same time, ensuring equitable treatment for similarly situated employees.

The Retention Assessment Matrix

As discussed in Chapter 14, retention risk is another area where an impact-probability matrix comes in handy. This is a good place for another 5 x 5 table, where one axis is the impact of the vacant role (role criticality), and along the other is the probability the incumbent will depart (risk of flight).

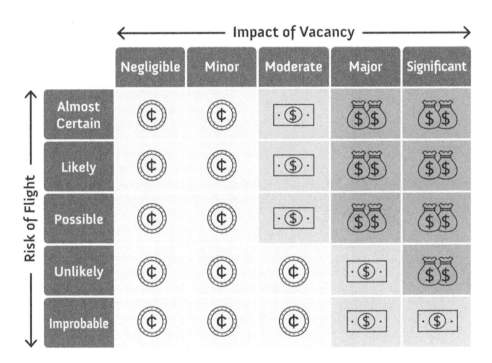

Sample Retention Assessment Matrix

Role Criticality (Impact)

A role is critical if it's necessary for meeting either short-term integration goals or longer-term business objectives. The sample matrix can help shape how HR practitioners consider the impact of a vacancy on these two considerations.

Role Criticality Ratings

Rating	Impact on Integration (Short-Term)	Impact on Operations (Long-Term)
5 (Significant)	The integration will not occur if the position is vacant.	The business cannot meet its mission. The role is part of succession planning.
4 (Major)	The vacancy will result in significant cost increases or schedule slips.	The business will miss critical financial objectives. The role is likely on a succession plan.
3 (Moderate)	Some cost increases will occur, and integration may be slightly delayed as a result of the vacancy.	The vacancy will impact customers. The role requires a skilled incumbent.
2 (Minor)	Other employees will experience some pain, but the team will find ways to work around the vacancy.	
1 (Negligible)	Very few people would notice the vacancy.	

Risk of Flight (Probability)

Flight risk attempts to measure the likelihood of a critical incumbent leaving for a different opportunity. The factors below are common indicators of an employee who is a flight risk. Each of these factors is worth one point, except for those related to compensation, which are worth two points. The scores are then totaled and placed on the heat map to assess flight risk.

Risk Factors:
- Will receive a significant payout when the deal closes (2 points).
- Total compensation is under market or perceived as under market (2 points).
- Has received other job offers (2 points).
- Low engagement or high stress, demonstrated by recent changes in work habits or attitudes and recent absenteeism, or signs of poor work-life balance like working excessive hours.
- Complicated manager relationships, including being turned down for a promotion.
- Challenging peer relationships or inability to bond with team members.
- Low tenure either at the company or in their current role.
- Known life changes or other personal factors.

Example: Ken is the IT manager of a company that is about to be acquired. He recently turned down a job offer because he has a great relationship with his manager and peers. However, Ken is starting to show signs of stress and is regularly working more than 40 hours a week. His wife is pregnant, and he's concerned about having time to bond with the new baby. In this scenario, Ken has a total of four points: two points for the job offers, one point for the stressful work conditions, and one point for the life change.

The table below represents the starting point for retention plans. Boxes with a cent (¢) are unlikely to require any retention, boxes with a dollar ($) suggest a moderate retention package, and boxes with money bags call for a significant retention package. The HR practitioner will need to exercise their best judgment and work closely with other stakeholders to determine the final retention plan for each employee.

Design Financial Incentives

To appropriately explore financial incentives, the HR practitioner will need to know about the payments the employees are already entitled to receive. To determine the right financial inducements, monies related to the acquisition as well as the employee's ongoing total rewards need to be considered. It can be hard to retain somebody who's just been made a millionaire if the retention package to get them to stick around is worth only $50,000! On the other hand, if the employee won't get a large payout and has a current pay package worth $70,000 a year, $20,000/year for the next three years can be very compelling.

The HR practitioner should receive a capitalization (or cap) table early in the due diligence process. The cap table shows who owns what portion of the acquired company. The spreadsheet includes equity information on investors, founders, advisors, employees, and others who have some claim to the company's assets in the event of a sale. The cap table should also include a waterfall analysis, which shows the payout each shareholder will receive when the company sells. The report will change when the parties agree on a final purchase price, but it is a valuable tool for estimating the effect of an individual retention package.

In addition to their equity payout from the business sale, some employees may be entitled to additional payments at change-in-control. These agreements are most common for executives or key employees in R&D or sales roles. Many acquirers request the seller waive these payments as a closing condition, but they may survive the transaction. In the US, these payments may carry 280G liabilities for "golden parachutes," so consultation with a tax expert may be required.

M&A Terms – Single and Double Triggers

To protect their future income, some employees negotiate payouts in the event of a business sale into their offers.

- **The first, or single, trigger is pulled when the business is sold.**

- **A double trigger is more complicated because the second trigger is not pulled unless the employee is terminated or downgraded as a result of the sale.**

The buyer will also need to be aware of any transaction bonuses the seller has promised employees. Boards authorize transaction bonuses to incentivize key leaders to sell all or part of the company. These bonuses can be substantial and may make retention more difficult post-close.

One additional factor to consider is any unvested equity that will transfer to the buyer alongside the employee. If the potential value of these holdings is sufficiently compelling, and vest at appropriate intervals, these prior equity holdings may be retentive. Analysis of the capitalization table and stock plans will help the HR practitioner understand which employees, if any, may be retained using this mechanism, which may have the added benefit of not incurring additional hard costs.

Shorter- or Longer-Term Retention: Delayed Deal Consideration

One of the most common mechanisms for retaining highly compensated key employees is the use of delayed deal consideration. In these arrangements, the acquirer promises to pay a portion of the deal proceeds at some future point. For example, a company may negotiate payment of 90% of what an executive is entitled to receive at close, with the remaining 10% held in escrow and paid out when the seller achieves specific revenue targets. Or, the buyer may offer to pay 70% of the CEO's equity payment at close, paying 15% after one year of service and the remaining 15% on the second anniversary date.

The parties frequently structure delayed consideration as either a holdback or earnout. While there are technical differences between these methods, the result is an increased ability to retain critical employees who are likely to receive deal payouts large enough to make more traditional incentive packages tough to design. Holdbacks and earnouts are not without complication. Sellers frequently complain that they no longer control the company, making it difficult for them to achieve the objectives required to earn the additional compensation. They may also feel that the acquirer is not providing accurate financial records, making it difficult to determine if they met their goals.

Shorter-Term Retention: Enhanced Severance

A generous severance package can provide an incentive to stay on board when the buyer only needs the employee's services for a limited duration. The employees may feel a sense of job security, at least in the short term, and believe they are financially protected while they search for another job.

A compelling severance package needs to provide compensation above the statutory or contractual amount the employee is already entitled to receive. Some companies choose to sweeten the pot by providing additional medical coverage during the severance period or offer outplacement services to assist the person in finding their next opportunity.

Enhanced severance plans may be less complicated for the acquirer to administer if there is a large workforce affected by the acquisition. The company can usually institute a policy change to manage the enhanced severance administratively. A company can also establish enhanced severance using individual agreements, which might be appropriate if the number of affected employees is small or if idiosyncratic arrangements are required.

One option to consider for smaller numbers of employees is accelerating equity payouts at the end of a transition period. Some firms allow an employee to remain on the payroll, but not have any formal work responsibility (a situation known as "garden leave" in some places) until their equity vests. In these "rest and vest" situations, the employees will need to complete specific tasks or transition critical knowledge before the garden leave commences.

Shorter-Term Retention: Integration Bonuses

Some employees need to perform work that goes above and beyond their day-to-day job responsibilities and require more incentive than an enhanced severance package may offer. In these situations, it is not uncommon to provide an integration bonus. These bonuses are designed to motivate the employee to complete specific tasks related to post-merger integration.

Companies typically pay integration bonuses at a specific point in time, such as three months post-close or one year after joining the acquirer's payroll. However, they may also design the plan such that payments are made only after certain milestones are accomplished, like the integration of a critical IT system or conversion of a certain number of customer contracts. Other integration bonuses may be tied to achieving precise business results, like meeting or exceeding targeted sales numbers.

Shorter-Term Retention: Consulting Arrangements

A potentially underutilized method for short-term retention of key talent is a consulting arrangement. In this situation, the former employee agrees to provide their services for a specific length of time or to complete certain tasks. This method can be helpful when the buyer or seller have concerns about taxes and flexibility. They can also be useful when the employee's services are only required on a part-time basis, as they allow the individual to take on additional work during the transitional time frame. The HR practitioner should consult with an attorney to ensure that they aren't accidentally creating a de facto employee relationship.

Longer-Term Retention: Increased Total Rewards

In some cases, increasing an employee's cash compensation in the form of either base pay or short-term incentives can provide sufficient financial incentive to stay on board. This step is appropriate if compensation analysis performed during due diligence shows employees are paid under market, and the raises bring them in alignment with market wages or the acquiring company's internal equity benchmarks.

Increases in total rewards can be compelling in the short-term for employees coming from start-up environments where equity is a significant part of their pay mix. When these employees move into an organization where ownership is not as substantial, or not available at all, increasing base pay helps the employee psychologically balance the "what might have been" of a grand payday if the start-up had gone with an IPO instead of an acquisition. Even when a company is crashing headlong toward bankruptcy, the psychological impact of losing what might have been must not be underestimated.

Longer-Term Retention: Cash or Equity Incentives

At times, the business believes they need specific individuals to stay on longer than the initial integration period to maximize their return on investment. In these cases, the buyer should contemplate longer-term incentive plans. Both cash and equity payments are common ways to provide long-term stay incentives for acquired employees.

When determining the mix of cash and equity, the firm's overall compensation philosophy must be considered. Some organizations will only pay in cash, others will only provide stock, and some choose a combination of the two. Equity payments have the advantage of aligning the employee to the acquirer's strategic objectives and overall financial success, but often have the disadvantage of being inflexible as they usually force the acquired employee into a preexisting stock plan.

When designing longer-term incentives, create a payment schedule that ensures the organization receives the best value for their money. Organizations typically provide longer-term incentives over two or three years with multiple payments made over that time frame. Some companies will choose to pay in equal installments every three, six, or twelve months. Other organizations will back-end load their payment schedule with a scheme that may pay 25% the first year, 25% the second year, and 50% at the end of year three.

If the organization is using the incentive to make up for lost income, such as a modified commission or bonus program that is effective on joining the acquirer's payroll, then the vesting schedule should allow the employee to maintain their current cash flow, while also creating an additional financial incentive to stay onboard and perform.

Discover Non-Financial Incentives

Non-financial incentives can be just as important as financial incentives when it comes to long-term retention. Determining non-financial incentives is more art than science, and often requires an understanding of the individual employee's motives. The good news is that there are some universal levers organizations can pull to drive retention. These include a compelling culture that fosters professional growth and development, demonstrated opportunities to lead exciting projects, and recognition for a job well done. These are essential elements of employee engagement, but leaders must communicate them effectively to retain acquired employees.

Many factors will be distinctive and require a one-on-one conversation with the employee. They include items like the span of control, expanded job titles, or even personal commitment to the existing team. To determine appropriate non-financial incentives, use a modified stay interview. If a critical-to-retain employee is not disclosed on the deal, their current manager may need to hold the stay interview and relay information back to the due diligence team.

The Society for Human Resource Management (SHRM) provides excellent guidance for stay interviews and offers several questions managers may want to ask their employees[3], including what they look forward to when coming to work, why they stay, what they would change, and what they aspire to achieve in their career. The business sponsor, corporate development team, and HR practitioner should use this approach to develop a dossier of each key employee's motivations to stay. They can then use this information to tailor a non-financial incentive package that is likely to meet the employee's needs and drive retention.

Create the Final Retention Package

Once the correct financial and non-financial incentives for the employee to stay have been determined, a final retention package needs to be created. In addition to addressing the financial and non-financial incentives for staying on board, the package should include details about the employee's future role with the organization. The package will likely include the same kind of information that will go into an offer letter, like job title, salary, and basic terms and conditions of employment.

The package will also need to be clear about what the employee must do to receive their retention incentives, including any milestones or metrics they must achieve. It should also detail the timing of incentive payments, and the form incentives will take, such as cash or stock, and any other conditions associated with the retention package. Some acquirers choose to include restrictive covenants such as non-compete, non-solicit, and non-disclosure agreements with the retention package.

Retention packages are often legal documents with arcane legalese. Employees can sometimes perceive retention documents as overly formal, and employees may have an adverse reaction to them. Some organizations work with their employment attorneys to create a more accessible cover letter for the documents, allowing the hiring manager or HR to extend a package that feels more friendly to the employee.

Communicate with Affected Employees

Key employees need to know they are critical as soon as possible. Leadership research by Bain & Company showed that successful acquirers quickly identify and assess critical employees, providing them with retention incentives within 30 days of announcement[4].

If key employees are aware of the acquisition, share their offer details as quickly as possible. If they aren't disclosed on the deal, be prepared to talk with them shortly after announcing the transaction. Extending the offers with urgency will help employees understand that they are essential, and knowing about the process that will be used to create their employment offer provides a sense of security.

Somebody from HR is going to talk to key employees the day the deal goes public. You get to choose if it's somebody from your HR team or somebody from your competitor's HR team. Determining the retention plan during the due diligence process is critical if you want to keep top performers around.

Part 5: Bringing It All Together

F rom the beginning of this book, we've stated that:

Due diligence is the art and science of identifying, assessing, and mitigating risks associated with an M&A transaction.

We have covered each of these elements separately. You now know how to identify risks using information that's available during each deal phase. You learned how to use a risk assessment matrix to determine the impact and probability associated with each risk. Finally, you learned several ways to mitigate risks that are unique to the M&A context. In this final part we will pull all of these elements together, showing you how to record risks and mitigation options.

Chapter 19: Developing Risk-Specific Mitigation Plans

At the end of Chapter 14, we showed a sample risk assessment matrix demonstrating the varying levels of information and different concerns that emerge in each phase of the due diligence process. The next step will be to develop specific mitigation options for each risk that emerges. We will use the same sample risk assessment matrix to show how this step is done.

Sample Risk Assessment Matrix

Probability \ Impact	Negligible	Minor	Moderate	Major	Significant
Almost Certain	⚠ 3.1	⚠	⊗ 2.1	⊗	⊗ 1.1
Likely	⚠	⚠	⚠ 2.2	⊗	⊗
Possible	✓	⚠	⚠ 2.3	⚠	⊗
Unlikely	✓	✓	⚠	⚠ 1.2	⚠
Improbable	✓	✓ 3.2	✓	⚠	⚠

Target Screening

The goal of the target screening phase is to determine whether the acquiring company will make a preliminary offer. Using the available public information and limited documents from the seller, the HR practitioner may find risks that can be mitigated using their full spectrum of options.

The HR practitioner's primary task during this phase is to identify deal killers and inputs to the financial model. This means their focus should be on risks that require killing the deal or making significant changes to the deal terms and conditions, including price and whether to pursue an asset or stock transaction. Executive retention should also be considered at this point, since it may be necessary to include the top-level retention information in the LOI.

If the HR practitioner finds risks that should be resolved during integration, those risks should be plotted onto the matrix, but not a lot of time should be spent thinking about them since at this point the deal might not go forward.

To see how this process works, look again at the sample risk assessment matrix. There are now some suggested mitigations to show how this process works.

- Risk 1.1: The target company CIM shows a retiree medical plan that is not adequately funded. It will cost $12M to fund the plan. The risk is almost certain and the impact is significant due to its total cost to remedy.

There are two likely mitigations for this risk. The first is to kill the deal since this type of risk is both significant and unavoidable. The second option may be a change the deal terms and conditions through a change to the purchase price or some kind of escrow to account for the underfunded liability. The business sponsor and corporate development team will make the final determination for this type of risk.

- Risk 1.2: Analysis of Glassdoor and social media mentions show the target company employees are motivated by their social values, which are expressed differently than the acquiring company's social values. It is possible, but unlikely, that the employees may choose to protest by quitting or organizing, which the company would consider a major impact. This challenge cannot be resolved using targeted retention incentives, so it is included in this risk matrix.

This risk is not a deal killer and is not likely to have a material economic impact on the initial deal model, meaning it is not relevant to the target screening phase. The HR practitioner should consider sharing the risk with the business sponsor and corporate development team so they are aware of it, but the most appropriate mitigation will be to leverage the integration plan by including this information in the overall change management approach.

Formal Due Diligence

While integration planning should start during the formal diligence phase, it's a good idea to prioritize risks that can only be mitigated by killing the deal, updating the financial model, or changing the definitive agreement. This is because once the deal is closed, the mitigation options become severely limited. Plans for retention of key employees not named in the LOI should also start early in the process.

In the example, the following risks emerged during formal due diligence:

- Risk 2.1: When discussing target company headcount with the finance team, the HR practitioner learns the synergy plan requires two factories to combine, resulting in job losses and triggering WARN notices. Additionally, one of the firm's major customers is in this town. The risk is almost certain to occur and it will take time and money to rebuild customer and employee trust.

This risk is not a deal killer, and since the buyer is choosing to combine the factories during integration, it's not appropriate to request a change to the definitive agreement. Depending on the severance implications, there is likely to be an impact to the deal financial model which should be calculated and shared with corporate development.

The best mitigation option for this risk is to work with other stakeholders to ensure the factory consolidation is handled in compliance with state and federal law, and leveraging the integration plan to ensure proper change management occurs.

- Risk 2.2: During the due diligence interview, the HR practitioner learns that one of the European locations is represented by a works council. After consulting with a labor attorney, they learn the works council must be consulted before the deal can go forward. The works council is likely to approve the plan, but will probably impose some conditions, making this risk likely to emerge. The labor expert assumes the deal timeline will slide one to two months, which is a moderate impact.

Risks like this will require multiple mitigation steps. First, the HR practitioner will probably need to change the deal terms and conditions to resolve this risk. The deal attorney and labor counsel will guide HR through changing the definitive agreement. Next, the HR practitioner will need to ensure the integration plan incorporates the possible delay to the deal timeline. Finally, they will want to ensure the change management plan incorporates requirements to consult with the works council.

- Risk 2.3: During the post-diligence huddle, the HR practitioner learns that attrition in the target's R&D department is twice as high as attrition in the acquirer's R&D department. If attrition continues at the current pace, and time to fill remains the same, critical R&D roles will be vacant for long periods of time, which may affect product release milestones. The risk is 40% likely to emerge, meaning the risk is possible. If the risk emerges, the impact will be moderate due to loss of customer trust and timeline challenges.

This type of risk underscores the importance of collaborating across functions to get a holistic view of the combined business. This is unlikely to be a deal killer and there is probably not a remedy available in the definitive agreement. This means the mitigation will be a combination of key talent retention (which should be covered on a different risk assessment matrix) and changes to the integration plan. The integration plan will include a mix of employee engagement interventions, change management, and recruiting. If any of the mitigation plans will result in significant extra expenses, the HR practitioner should share their estimates with the corporate development team so they can incorporate them into the deal financial model.

Integration Planning

After the deal is signed and announced, the primary focus changes to planning the integration process so the deal can provide positive financial results. There is a chance that a significant issue that could be a deal killer will be uncovered, but that is unlikely. The HR practitioner will also continue to look for items with a financial impact.

In the example, the following information was found after the deal was signed.

- Risk 3.1: When job descriptions were reviewed, it was discovered that the office manager in one location is probably misclassified under the FLSA. Back wages will be approximately $10,000. This risk is almost certain to occur, but the cost is negligible in the overall context of the deal.

Risks like this one will almost certainly emerge as the due diligence process continues. While the dollar value is small in context, any time a compliance risk needs to be mitigated, consulting an attorney who will help decide the correct next steps is recommended.

- Risk 3.2: During a conversation with the target's HR leader, the HR practitioner learns the target cannot find intellectual property agreements for several back-office employees. The risk of an issue emerging is improbable since the employees did not work directly on any products and did not have access to trade secrets. The impact of an issue arising would be minor for the same reason.

Risks that appear in the lower left quadrant of the risk assessment matrix may not require a mitigation at all. If a mitigation is required for this risk, it's best to work with an intellectual property attorney to decide the correct next steps. In this case, the HR practitioner may ask the target to get agreements from each employee or leverage the integration plan by requiring the employees to execute a new agreement after the deal closes.

If this risk had emerged during the formal due diligence phase, it may have been decided to change the deal terms to require the target to get each employee to execute an agreement as a closing condition.

Integration and Value Capture

After the deal has closed, the HR practitioner's responsibility shifts from due diligence to integration. The goal of integration is to help the company achieve the strategic and financial goals that drove the deal to start with. Creating the integration plan is outside of the scope of this book, but be sure that every item identified for mitigation through the integration plan carries into the actual project plan.

Once the deal is closed, mitigation options are very limited and will generally involve adjustments to the integration plan or a common-sense HR intervention. If the HR practitioner finds an issue that is particularly egregious, like a significant misrepresentation or outright lie from the seller, they should work with the corporate development team to see if it is appropriate to make a claim against the escrow or enforce an indemnity clause.

Chapter 20: Communicating Due Diligence Findings

The first two phases of the due diligence process provide unique opportunities to share HR findings with the business sponsor and corporate development team. If an acquiring organization has a specific format for sharing a target screening brief or due diligence report, the HR practitioner should follow it. If the firm does not, this chapter will help HR practitioners develop tools and templates they can use for their deals. A version is also available at the HR M&A Roundtable website (www.MandARoundtable.com)

Target Screening Brief

During the target screening phase, business sponsors and corporate development are deciding if they are interested enough in the target company to make an offer and what the proposed purchase price should be. The LOI will often delineate how top executives will be treated, as that information can be critical for helping the seller decide if a buyer is right for them.

At this point, the HR practitioner will have very limited data, consisting only of public information, the CIM, and anything else the seller has provided. Some companies will have a preliminary integration model at this point, which HR should also keep in mind when completing the brief.

HR will be operating off limited data, but should consider providing analysis related to each of the major sections listed below.

- HR's opinion about proceeding with the deal.
    - Are there any HR-related deal killers? Remember, HR deal killers are rare.
    - Is there any reason to prefer a share sale over an asset sale or vise-versa?

- A summary of information about the organization, including:
  o Approximate headcount
  o Key locations
  o Critical workforce capabilities
  o Any HR-related differentiators
- Top executives who should be specifically named in the LOI. The list is usually created in partnership with business sponsors and corporate development.
  o A brief biography of each top executive.
  o Key financial and non-financial elements of the retention proposal.
- If preliminary synergy plans have been developed, HR's assessment of the risks, issues, and opportunities associated with the synergy plans.
- A synopsis of key cultural characteristics that can be inferred from public information.
  o Any important cultural similarities and differences that are emerging.
  o How cultural similarities and differences will affect integration and value capture.

During this stage, information that will be important during formal due diligence or integration planning may be found. The HR practitioner should hang on to this information in case the deal moves forward.

Formal Due Diligence Report

The formal due diligence phase is mainly used to identify potential deal killers, provide inputs to the financial model, and propose changes to the definitive agreement. The financial model includes deal synergies, which HR may help to validate during the formal diligence phase. HR will also start working on retention of key employees.

The due diligence report is usually a multi-page document that provides critical information on people, leadership, and culture to business sponsors, corporate development, and the integration management office. The list below includes key sections to consider including in this report.

- Update HR's opinion about proceeding with the deal.
  - Are there any HR-related deal killers? Remember, HR deal killers are rare.
  - Is there any reason to prefer a share sale over an asset sale or vise-versa?
- A summary of the proposed synergy plans and integration model and how it will affect people, leadership, and culture.
- A list of key employees to retain. The list is usually created in partnership with business sponsors and corporate development.
  - A brief summary of each employee's capabilities and why they are being retained.
  - Key financial and non-financial elements of the retention proposal.
- Updated information about the organization, including the effects of the integration plan.
  - Current organizational structure along with any proposed changes to the organization.
  - Current headcount and any changes that might occur as a result of the integration, including costs related to severance and recruiting if that is part of the plan.
  - Key locations, including costs related to transferring employees if that is part of the plan.
  - Critical workforce capabilities, including costs related to training employees if that is part of the plan.
  - Any HR-related differentiators that should be included in the organizational analysis.
- Other HR information that may be included in the cost model.
  - Cost impact of changes to total rewards, including the side-by-side analysis.
  - Cost impact of changes to the HR service delivery model.
- A summary of key HR practices, including any significant compliance risks.

- An update to the synopsis of key cultural characteristics.
  - Any important cultural similarities and differences that are emerging.
  - How cultural similarities and differences will affect integration and value capture.
  - A summary of significant cultural barriers to implementing the preliminary integration model.
- HR's assessment of other risks, issues, and opportunities associated with the proposed synergy plans or integration models that have not already been captured.

During the formal diligence phase, HR practitioners may run across information that is not relevant to the business sponsor or corporate development team, but is relevant to the HR function. HR practitioners should keep this information handy, as it may be useful when shaping and implementing the integration plan.

Conclusion

As we.ve discussed throughout this book, buying a company is a lot like buying a home. This book covered the first half of that process. We started with target screening, which is a lot like house hunting. We covered the most common strategic goals for firms doing M&A, along with common ways of structuring transactions.

Buying A House

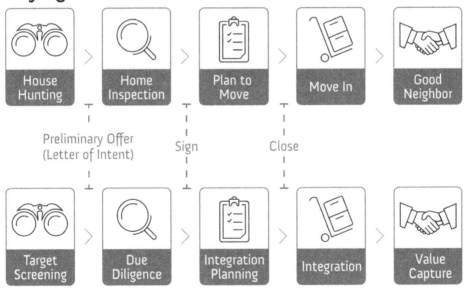

Buying A Company

Formal diligence, our M&A home inspection, comes next and was the focus on this book. Using this book as a guide, you can now identify, assess, and work to mitigate the common people, leadership, and culture risks associated with an M&A transaction. You have the tools to quantify these risks in every phase of a deal, and know how to communicate the risks and mitigations to your most important stakeholders.

You also learned about the information ecosystem, including where you can go to gather facts about the target company at different points in the deal. You know how to compile data to get a clearer picture of the people, leadership, and culture in the target company.

Combining what you learned in this book with your professional instincts will equip you to successfully manage your next M&A due diligence process.

What Comes Next?

Just like a homeowner can't knock down walls until they have the keys to the house, an acquirer can't make changes to an acquired company until the deal is closed. Post-Merger Integration typically touches the entire workforce, making HR engagement critical to success.

Post-Merger Integration is outside of the scope of this book, but you won't have to do that step alone either. The HR M&A Roundtable is a network of people who care about the people, leadership, and culture aspects of M&A. We offer a variety of free and paid options to improve your skills as an HR M&A practitioner, including face-to-face roundtables in major cities, virtual roundtables, high-quality training, and an annual conference. To learn more about us, visit our website at www.MandARoundtable.com.

My Best Advice

A few years ago, I gave a presentation on HR due diligence at HR West, one of the largest HR conferences in the United States. During the Q&A portion of my presentation, a seasoned HR practitioner stood up and said, "I'm overwhelmed. There is so much to do. What is the one thing I should focus on?"

I took a moment to think and replied, "The most important thing isn't on any of my slides. The most important thing to focus on is trusting your instincts. You are an experienced HR practitioner and your leadership would not have given you this job if they didn't think you were up for it. Trust yourself!"

I'm giving you the same advice: *Trust Yourself!*

You can do this and the HR M&A Roundtable is available to help if you need us.

Acknowledgements

Just like successful M&A work requires the efforts of an entire group of people, writing a book is also a team sport. *The HR Practitioner's Guide to Mergers & Acquisitions Due Diligence* would not have come together without the contributions of a magnificent community of people committed to making M&A work for everybody.

Words cannot express my gratitude to the amazing people who work in and around M&A, many of whom gave their time and expertise to ensure this book is useful for HR practitioners. If you find this guide useful as you find yourself face-to-face with one of the most challenging events in your profession, working on a deal, I hope you join me in thanking these individuals for their contributions.

Brenda Hastings, my friend and Executive Director of the HR M&A Roundtable, is a talented HR professional who brought a common-sense HR perspective to this entire project.

Both the HR M&A Roundtable community and this book have benefitted greatly from Steve Steckler, who has co-chaired our conferences and Keeley Mooneyhan who generously provided the blueprint for successful roundtable meetings. Along with many others, they helped me shape my thoughts on due diligence so I could share them with our community.

Many members and friends of the HR M&A Roundtable lent their wisdom, expertise, and encouragement to this project as well. Roundtable Intern Brendan McElroy did the heavy lifting on cultural assessment. Drs. Marc Prine and Keith Dunbar offered meaningful insight into M&A leadership. Mark Walztoni gave his thoughts on retention. Entrepreneur Kison Patel of the M&A Science podcast and DealRoom has continued to selflessly give to the M&A community and this endeavor.

Klint C. Kendrick

The fact that this book is not 200 pages of gibberish is largely due to the efforts of my book coach, Suzanne Doyle-Ingram, who helped ensure the book was organized from the start and my editor, Darcy Jayne, who ensured a consistent tone and voice throughout. Thanks also go to Scott Allen, who ensured the visuals supported the key learnings.

Finally, this book would not have been possible without the support and encouragement of my husband, Scott Lindauer, who endured many weekends and evenings of being chased out of my work area while I clicked away at the keyboard. Thanks also go to my children, Koyle, Kayden, Kaleb, and McKenna, and their mom, Sarah-Anne, for continually inspiring me to do my part in making the world a better place for their sake.

About the Author

Klint Kendrick has worked in human resources for over two decades, with extensive experience in mergers and acquisitions, international HR, people analytics, total rewards, workforce planning, diversity and inclusion, employee engagement, recruitment and retention. Dr. Kendrick has worked in multiple environments, ranging from HR leadership roles at Fortune 500 companies like Oracle and Boeing to being an HR department of one for scrappy start-ups.

Klint holds a Ph.D. in Organizational Leadership and a master's degree in Industrial/Organizational Psychology from The Chicago School of Professional Psychology, an MBA from California State, and an undergraduate degree in business from Eastern Oregon University. He holds designations as a Six Sigma Green Belt, Senior Professional in Human Resources (SPHR), and Senior Certified Professional by the Society for Human Resource Management (SHRM-SCP).

Organizations like The Conference Board, Bloomberg BNA, Thomson Reuters, McKinsey, Mercer, Willis Towers Watson, Transaction Advisors, MergerWare, Midaxo, and DealRoom have invited Klint to share his insights on the human side of M&A. Post-event surveys show that audiences find Klint friendly, engaging, and knowledgeable. They appreciate how his highly interactive style drives both conceptual learning and practical application.

Dr. Kendrick is a firm believer in professional development, and has worked to ensure HR professionals can benefit from formal training, mentoring, and peer-learning. Klint has started HR M&A Roundtables in Seattle, Chicago, and online, and chairs an annual conference for HR professionals working on mergers and acquisitions. His work has inspired other roundtables to start in Dallas, New York and London. You can learn more about the roundtables at www.MandARoundtable.com.

About the HR M&A Roundtable

The HR M&A Roundtable is a peer-learning forum for Human Resource professionals working on mergers and acquisitions. We provide a safe and confidential environment where members share their lessons learned and best practices. The roundtable is not associated with any outside company, but is driven by its practitioner members.

Dr. Klint Kendrick started the HR M&A Roundtable after several HR practitioners noted that our unique organizational cultures and the very nature of our work make it difficult to pilot new ways of supporting our organizations and acquired employees. This makes HR M&A an ideal discipline for roundtable learning.

Members are encouraged to share openly, but are required to honor their non-disclosure agreements and other professional obligations. No confidential or sensitive information may be shared with the roundtable. To encourage open sharing, roundtable meetings operate under the Chatham House Rule, where participants may make use of the information shared by their fellow members, but they may not share the identity or affiliation of any speakers or members.

The HR M&A Roundtable offers a variety of free and paid programming, including face-to-face roundtables in New York, Chicago, Dallas, and London. Virtual offerings include regular webinars, structured roundtable discussions, and networking happy hours. The roundtable also hosts an annual conference, where participants gather for two days to network and learn from one another.

For more information about joining the HR M&A Roundtable, visit www.MandARoundtable.com.

References

Introduction

[1] Maxwell, J.C. (2008). *Leadership Gold: Lessons I've Learned from a Lifetime of Leading.* New York: HarperCollins.

Part 1: M&A Basics

[1] Hyatt, J. (2019, June 30). *The new deals: The changing state of M&A activity.* The Wall Street Journal, Deloitte CFO Journal.

[2] Krouskos, S. (2019, October 14). *Why global M&A is expected to remain healthy into 2020.* EY.com.

Chapter 1: The Deal Lifecyle

[1] Bright, P. (2011, May 10). *Microsoft buys Skype. Why, exactly?* Wired.

[2] Brion, R. (2012, June 4). *Starbucks buys SF bakery chain La Boulange for $100M.* Eater.

[3] Palmieri, M. (2015, December 10). *TruGreen, Scotts LawnService to merge.* Landscape Management.

Chapter 2: Strategic Basis for M&A

[1] Harding. D. & Rouse, T. (April 2007). *Human due diligence.* Harvard Business Review.

[2] Burnett, G. M. (2020, January 10). *Analysis: U.S. M&A Mega Year in Review.* Bloomberg Law Analysis.

[3] Noether, M., May, S., & Stearns, B. (2019, September). *Hospital merger benefits: Views from hospital leaders and econometric analysis – an update.* American Hospital Association.

[4] Charter Communications. (2015, May 26). *Charter to merge with Time Warner Cable and acquire Bright House Networks: Combinations benefit shareholders, consumers and cable industry.*

[5] Heine, F. (2012, February 2). *K&L Gates merges with Italian indie to launch in Milan.* Law.com.

[6] Lunden, I. (2017, December 4). *Chase closes WePay acqusition, a deal valued up to $400M.* TechCrunch.

[7] Green, D. (2019, June 13). *Walmart's $3.3 billion acquisition of Jet.com is still the foundation on which all of its e-commerce dreams are built.* Business Insider.

[8] Lerner, M. (2018, August 23). *Excess capacity sets reinsurers up for consolidation: S&P.* Business Insurance.

[9] Reisenger, D. (2015, November 13). *Apple is shutting down Beats Music, just like most companies it buys.* Fortune.

[10] Meckl, R. & Röhrle, F. (2016). *Do M&A deals create or destroy value? A meta-analysis.* European Journal of Business and Economics.

[11] Martin, R. L. (June 2016). *M&A: The one thing you need to get right.* Harvard Business Review.

[12] Harding. D. & Rouse, T. (April 2007). *Human due diligence.* Harvard Business Review.

[13] Tortoriello, R., Oyeniyi, T., Pope, D., Fruin, P., & Falk, R. (August 2016). *Mergers & Acquisitions: The good, the bad, and the ugly (and how to tell them apart).* S&P Global Market Intelligence.

[14] Lewis, A. & McKone, D. (2016, May 10). *So many M&A deals fail because companies overlook this simple strategy.* Harvard Business Review.

[15] Chartier, J., Liu, A., Raberger, N., & Silva, R. (2018). *Seven rules to crack the code on revenue synergies in M&A.* McKinsey & Company.

[16] Hayward, M. L. A., & Hambrick, D. C. (1997). *Explaining the premiums paid for large acquisitions: Evidence of CEO hubris.* Administrative Science Quarterly, 42*(1), 103–127.*

[17] Jensen, M. C., & Murphy, K. J. (1990). *Performance pay and top-management incentives.* Journal of Political Economy, 98(2), 225-264.

[18] Cartwright, S. & Cooper, C.L. (1992). *Mergers & acquisitions: The human factor.* Oxford: Butterworth-Heinemann Ltd.

[19] Milano, C. (2015, September 1). *Bad influence: How well connected CEOs impact M&A results.* Risk Management.

[20] Berkshire Hathaway Inc. (2014). *2014 Shareholder Letter.*

[21] Viguerie, P., Smit, S., & Baghai, M. (2008). *The granularity of growth: How to identify the sources of growth and drive enduring company performance.* Hoboken, NJ: Wiley.

[22] Rusignola, D. (2019 May/June). *How the new Weyerhaeuser CEO keeps the timberland REIT rooted in its values.* REIT Magazine.

[23] Weisberg, L. (2009, October 8). *SeaWorld parks sold in $2.7 billion deal.* The San Diego Union-Tribune.

[24] Yang, R. (2020, January 8). *After a string of divestments, can Campbell Soup resume its growth path?* The Motley Fool.

[25] Kendall, B. (2015, January 27). *FTC clears Safeway-Albertsons Merger.* Wall Street Journal.

[26] Harding, D. & Rovit, S. (2004, November 15). *Writing a credible investment thesis.* Harvard Business Review.

[27] Patel, K. (2019). *Agile M&A: Proven techniques to close deals faster and maximize value. A practitioner's guide.* USA: Day1 Inc.

Chapter 3: What Makes Deals Work – Or Not

[1] Burnett, G. M. (2020, January 10). *Analysis: U.S. M&A Mega Year in Review.* Bloomberg Law Analysis.

[2] PWC. (2019). *Deals 2020 outlook: Making bold M&A deals during times of rapid change.*

[3] Iger, R. (2019, September 18). *"We could say anything to each other": Bob Iger remembers Steve Jobs, the Pixar drama, and the Apple merger that wasn't.* Vanity Fair.

[4] Barnes, B. & Cieply, M. (2009, August 31). *Disney swoops into action, buying Marvel for $4 billion.* New York Times.

[5] Kovach, St. (2012, October 30). *Disney buys Lucasfilm for $4 billion.* Business Insider.

[6] Berkowitz, J. (2019, December 16). *Disney's dominance of the 2019 box office means its takeover of movies is complete.* Fast Company.

[7] Callham, J. (2018, July 11). *Google made its best acquisition 13 years ago: Can you guess what it was?* Android Authority.

[8] Eadicicco, L. (2015, March 27). *The rise of Android: How a flailing startup became the world's biggest computing platform.* Business Insider.

[9] Young, J. (2012, April 23). *Want Google to buy your startup? Think a bit more like Google.* Financial Post.

[10] Corcoran, G. (2010, November 30). *Exxon-Mobil 12 years later: Archetype of a successful deal.* The Wall Street Journal.

[11] Stempel, J. (2009, January 1). *Bank of America completes Merrill Lynch purchase.* Reuters.

[12] Moore, H. N. (2009, April 20). *Bank of America & Merrill Lynch: Now, about that integration.* Wall Street Journal.

[13] French, K. (2008, November 14). *Update: 6,200 Merrill Fas sign BofA retention at deadline.* Wealth Management.

[14] Byrne, J. A. (2015, April 4). *Bank of America accused of 'tarnishing' Merrill Lynch.* New York Post.

15 Horowitz, J. (2019, February 25). *Bank of America is phasing out the 105-year-old Merrill Lynch brand.* CNN Business.

[16] Finkelstein, S. (2009, March 3). *Why Ken Lewis destroyed Bank of America.* Forbes.

[17] Reeves, J. (2013, September 14). *3 troubling questions about Bank of America's epic acquisition of Merrill Lynch.* The Motley Fool.

[18] Tully, S. (2009, January 30). *Divorce – Bank of America style.* CNN Money.

[19] Rothacker, R. (2014, August 17). *The deal that cost Bank of America $50 billion – and counting.* Charlotte Observer.

[20] Andrews, E. L. & Holson, L. M. (2001, August 12). *Daimler-Benz to buy Chrysler in $36 billion deal.* New York Times.

[21] Finkelstein, A. (1995, April 12). *Chrysler takeover bid leaves workers nervous, glad Iacocca's involved.* AP News.

[22] McGarry, D. (2000, November 18). *DaimlerChrysler's culture clash.* MarketWatch.

[23] Maynard, M. (2007, August 12). *DAM-lerChrysler? If you say so, chief.* The New York Times.

[24] McGrath, R. G. (2015, January 10). *15 years later, lessons from the failed AOL-Time Warner merger.* Fortune.

[25] Dealbook. (2010, January 11). *How the AOL-Time Warner deal went wrong.* New York Times.

[26] Surowiecki, J. (2003, January 20). *The culture excuse.* The New Yorker.

[27] Feloni, R. (2018, October 13). *Billionaire investor Steve Case says the failure of the 2000 AOL Time Warner mega merger taught him a crucial lesson about execution.* Business Insider.

[28] Surowiecki, J. (2003, January 20). *The culture excuse.* The New Yorker.

[29] Peers, M. & Angwin, J. (2000, December 8). *AOL, Time Warner plan stock options for all employees of combined firm.* The Wall Street Journal.

[30] Carlson, N. (2009, November 16). *AOL spinoff set for December 9.* Business Insider.

Chapter 6: HR Topics

[1] U.S. Securities and Exchange Commission (2019). *Proposed Rule: Modernization of regulation S-K items 101, 103, and 105.* Washington, D.C.

[2] Naden, C. (2019, January 15). *New ISO international standard for human capital reporting.* International Standards Organization.

[3] Engagement Strategies Media (2019). *First ISO human capital standards now available.*

Part 3: Identifying and Assessing HR Risks

[1] Harding. D. & Rouse, T. (April 2007). *Human due diligence.* Harvard Business Review.

Chapter 11: Leadership Risk

[1] Deloitte. (2013, November 18). *Leadership in M&A: Capabilities for successful deal outcomes.* The Wall Street Journal, Deloitte CFO Journal.

[2] Dubner, S.J, (2018, March 4). *Extra: David Rubenstein full interview.* Freakonomics radio podcast.

[3] Dunbar, J. K. (2014, September). *The leaders who make M&A work.* Harvard Business Review.

[4] Ulrich, D. & Allen, J. (2017, August 11). *PE firms are creating a new role: Leadership capital partner.* Harvard Business Review.

[5] Alexander, K. & Davis, R. (2017, August). *A view from both sides: How PE firms and sellers can form wise partnerships* [Industry Research Report]. Kilberry.

[6] Abel, A. L., Devine, M. & Dunbar, J. K., (2019). *The leadership factor in mergers & acquisitions* [Research Report 1684-19]. The Conference Board.

Chapter 12: Culture Risk

[1] Cartwright, S. & Cooper, C.L. (1992). *Mergers & acquisitions: The human factor.* Oxford: Butterworth-Heinemann Ltd.

[2] Tibergian, M. (2018, June 27). *Does culture really matter in M&A?* ThinkAdvisor.

[3] McElroy, B. (2020). Unpublished research on culture in M&A.

[4] Hollingsworth, J. (2016, October 28). *Culture clash: why western companies are better at mergers than their Chinese and Japanese counterparts.* South China Morning Post.

Chapter 15: Kill the Deal

[1] Parker, R. (2016, September 16). *Half of all business sales fall apart in due diligence, here's what to do.* Forbes.

Chapter 18: Provide Retention Incentives

[1] Walztoni, M. (2016). Blending cultures: success factors in merging knowledge-based companies. In M. Finney (Ed.) HR directions: HR leading lights on what you should know right now about leadership, engagement, technology, and growing your own world-class HR career (pp. 169-184). Santa Fe, NM: HR C-Suite.

[2] Krug, J. and Shill, W. (2008), The big exit: executive churn in the wake of M&As, Journal of Business Strategy, Vol. 29 No. 4, pp. 15-21.

[3] Finnegan, R (2018, August 13). *How to conduct stay interviews: Core features and advantages.* Society for Human Resource Management.

[4] Harding. D. & Rouse, T. (April 2007). *Human due diligence.* Harvard Business Review.

Printed in Great Britain
by Amazon

65745337R00102